Boundless Love

Boundless Love

A Companion to Clark H. Pinnock's Theology

ANDREW RAY WILLIAMS

Foreword by Daniel Castelo

WIPF & STOCK · Eugene, Oregon

BOUNDLESS LOVE
A Companion to Clark H. Pinnock's Theology

Wipf & Stock
An Imprint of Wipf and Stock Publishers
199 W. 8th Ave., Suite 3
Eugene, OR 97401

www.wipfandstock.com

PAPERBACK ISBN: 978-1-7252-8652-8
HARDCOVER ISBN: 978-1-7252-8653-5
EBOOK ISBN: 978-1-7252-8654-2

07/14/21

To Chris E.W. Green,
for your investment and friendship

Contents

Foreword

I HAVE ALWAYS BEEN impressed with those who out of their love for God blaze a path that does not fit regnant paradigms. It is not that these figures do so in order to be nonconformists; they simply follow God, come what may. These figures are often activists; at times they are pastors. And every now and then, they are theologians. Those in the latter camp are a rare breed indeed, especially given how the academy often incentivizes the perpetuation of the status quo. But they do exist, and Clark Pinnock is one such case.

Pinnock seemed to wander where he felt led and was willing to question and upend the conventional thinking of his surroundings. That he did so implies a certain boldness, a kind of confidence many of us only wish we could muster. That boldness and confidence, however, were grounded in a deep form of devotion—one that comes through on occasion in his writings. For me personally, I have not always agreed where Pinnock landed, especially as it relates to some of his metaphysical proposals and his evaluation of certain voices from the Christian tradition. And yet, I knew his views flowed from a serious and sincere love for God. Given the goodness of that posture, I cannot help but think that an engagement with *this* kind of theologian merits a bit of delicacy and grace. If only his critics—especially his evangelical critics—would concede the point.

Given how difficult he is to categorize and yet how impactful his work has been, Pinnock should be extensively studied today. Williams laments that for many students today, their introduction to Pinnock is mediated through various critical voices. That is unfortunate because it bespeaks an impoverished form of theological reasoning—that a critical mediation would allow a figure to be well-represented. Return to the sources! *Ad fontes!* And as one does, guides such as Williams' *Boundless Love* can prove helpful in contextualizing the arguments, collating the relevant literature, and providing some summary guidance in how to navigate it all. Williams has done us all a great service in lifting up the profile of this generative and "controversial" theologian.

Daniel Castelo, PhD
William Kellon Quick Professor of Theology and Methodist Studies
Duke Divinity School

Acknowledgments

Like many things in my life, the opportunity to write this book is a result of the kindness and support of others. This book has been dramatically improved thanks to the many suggestions and corrections of friends. Thanks to Bradford McCall, Daniel Isgrigg, David Bradnick, and David Ray Johnson for their constructive feedback on early drafts of these chapters. Of course, any deficiencies remain completely my responsibility. I also want to thank Thomas Jay Oord for his help in locating some of Pinnock's unpublished works and for his early encouragement in the project. Many thanks to Steven Félix-Jäger for providing the custom artwork for the book's cover. I also want to acknowledge the church I claim the joy of pastoring—Family Worship Center—for their love and trust. Thanks to my brother, Nathan Williams, for reading several drafts of chapters and providing helpful feedback for revision. Many thanks to my parents, Brandon Williams and Pamela Beverage, who from a young age provided me with rich faith and an interest in theological matters. I am also incredibly grateful for my wife, Anna, not only for her constant encouragement, but for providing me the time to research and write. Most of all, though, I am thankful for Anna's commitment and love. My incredible daughters, Adelaide and Audrey also deserve many thanks for their sacrifices in time with me as I wrote this book. Finally, I am grateful to Chris E. W. Green for his mentorship and for his early encouragement in the project. This work is dedicated to you, my friend.

Introduction

WHO WAS CLARK PINNOCK?

Often known among evangelicals as an early proponent of "open theism" or the "open view of God," Clark Pinnock (1937–2010) was arguably one of the most noted, productive, and provocative Christian theologians in North American evangelical Christianity in the late twentieth century. As Roger Olson has remarked, "Clark Pinnock pioneered a new way of being an evangelical in theology," making him one of the most significant and controversial Evangelical voices in recent history. Though Pinnock began his theological career as a conservative Calvinist, he concluded it as a "post-conservative" freewill theist, who often engaged in discussions with Wesleyan, Pentecostal, and Process theologians.

Early in his career, Pinnock became an influential figure in the Southern Baptist Convention's (SBC) battles over biblical inerrancy. As a result of his time teaching at New Orleans Baptist Theological Seminary (1965–69), many of Pinnock's students became leaders in the "conservative resurgence" or "fundamentalist takeover" of the SBC. After moving to Trinity Evangelical Divinity School (Deerfield, IL), then to Regent College (Vancouver, BC), and finally to McMaster Divinity College (Hamilton, ON), Pinnock's views on Scripture and inerrancy changed. In fact, Pinnock changed his mind throughout his career on several significant issues. However, as he describes it, "I have changed mainly in one way not in many."[1] Pinnock shares that he underwent a paradigm shift, beginning in the early 1970s that played itself out over three decades. As he puts it, "It was a shift in the doctrine of God which saw me gradually move from the root metaphor of God as an absolute monarch to the root metaphor of God as a loving Parent. It was an important change which would affect a whole range of issues as its significance worked itself out."[2]

Though once emphasizing a Calvinistic view of God's sovereignty, Pinnock gradually embraced a theology giving an equal or greater weight to human free will. As Steven Studebaker has noted, though Pinnock "retained a strong association with evangelicalism," he "also sought to move beyond both its experiential and theological framework."[3] Due to this, Pinnock's work often stirred tensions within conventional, conservative Evangelical theology. This was especially true of his contribution in *The Openness of God* (1994). While Pinnock began receiving invitations from Wesleyan and Pentecostal scholarly societies around this time,[4] Pinnock was nearly kicked out of the more conservative Evangelical Theological Society. In 2002, members of the society voted 388 to 231 to retain him as a member in good standing.[5] In reflecting upon his evangelical credentials being called into question, Pinnock said, "I have difficulty with that interpretation. I thought it was fairly clear from my conversion, my walk in the Spirit, my life of prayer, my love of the Bible, my respect for tradition, my efforts in apologetics, my work in evangelism. I wonder what I would have to do to prove it?"[6]

Despite Pinnock's mixed reception, however, he continued to nevertheless produce significant works of theology throughout his career. His 1996 Magnum Opus, *Flame of Love: A Theology of the Holy Spirit* has been deemed, by some, to be "one of the most significant evangelical theologies produced in the last decade of the twentieth

1. Pinnock, "Response to Daniel Strange and Amos Yong," 351.

2. Pinnock, "Response to Daniel Strange and Amos Yong," 351.

3. Studebaker, *From Pentecost*, 200.

4. Around this time, Pinnock began interacting with the Wesleyan Theological Society as well as the Society for Pentecostal Studies.

5. Allen, "Baptist Theologian Clark Pinnock Dies," 18.

6. Pinnock, "Response to Daniel Strange and Amos Yong," 352.

century."[7] Pinnock's innovative, ecumenical, and constructive approach to evangelical theology was as fresh as it was exploratory. Pinnock was undaunted by utilizing many sources in his theological pursuit, for example. As Thomas Jay Oord has stated of Pinnock, he thought the "best theology can draw from diverse sources, while keeping a coherence amidst generative differences."[8] Pinnock's final monograph, *Most Moved Mover: A Theology of Openness* (2001),[9] reflects this exploratory and ecumenical framework, as well. In this title, Pinnock aimed to re-represent the open view of God "in light of many useful criticisms and a few fresh reflections,"[10] by dialoguing with fresh readings of Scripture and by evoking ecumenical interchange.

WHAT IS THE PURPOSE OF THE BOOK?

To briefly mention a personal reminiscence, I first encountered Pinnock's theology in seminary when my professor assigned reading in Pinnock's *Flame of Love*. As a Pentecostal, I was both surprised and pleased by his positive remarks regarding Pentecostal and charismatic spirituality/theology. Almost instantaneously, I became one of many Pentecostals who had "somewhat of a love affair with Pinnock and his *Flame of Love*."[11] It has been said that "as a charismatic evangelical, Pinnock has been a catalyst and a role model for Pentecostal theologians who endeavor to develop unique contributions to theology, which are free from the cloister of conservative evangelical theology."[12] Personally, I have found Pinnock's eclectic, ecumenical, and enthusiastic style exhilarating, both as a fledging student and now as a professional theologian. My overall evaluation of Pinnock's contribution to contemporary theology is strongly positive. Indeed,

7. Studebaker, "Integrating Pneumatology," 5.

8. Oord, "Clark Pinnock."

9. *Most Moved Mover* was a published collection of Pinnock's Disbury Lectures, delivered at Nazarene Theological College, Manchester, England (October, 2000).

10. Pinnock, *Most Moved Mover*, 9.

11. Swoboda, *Tongues and Trees*, 86, fn 118.

12. Studebaker, *From Pentecost*, 200.

though I find some developments within his theology problematic, and some ideas open to serious criticism, I have great affinity for the nature and overall direction of Pinnock's theological endeavor.

Over the years, however, I have discovered that first-time readers of Pinnock often do not encounter his theology on its own terms, as I did. Rather, evangelical students, for instance, are often first introduced to Pinnock through secondary sources, which are often quite critical of his positions. In fact, my initial suppositions have been solidified even further as I have spoken with various seminary students who recounted to me their first introduction to Pinnock. In my most recent conversation, I quickly recognized that the only exposure this student had to Pinnock's theology was through conservative evangelical texts, decrying the heretical nature of Pinnock's overall project. Not only did this interaction sadden me—considering how different it was from my initial encounter with Pinnock's work—but it prompted me once again to question whether the "big tent" evangelicalism that Pinnock championed and envisioned is all but gone. Still, I imagine that if Pinnock were still alive, he would continue to consider his pursuit of an ecumenical theology a "worthwhile" endeavor, despite all of the "opposition."[13]

This book, then, is an attempt to give Pinnock a fresh and fair hearing, outlining some of his major themes, while also providing an accessible point of entry into his theology. While I will focus upon Pinnock's thought in detail, I will at times compare Pinnock's thought to other theologians with whom he agrees, while also noting those with whom he disagrees. It is my hope that this will help provide some context to "locate" Pinnock within the landscape of twentieth century Western theology. Perhaps, though, I should say a few words about what this book is *not*. It is not my intent to deliver an exhaustive introduction to Pinnock. I sidestep the customary discussion of biography and avoid providing anything resembling an intellectual history. Barry Callen's work, *Clark H. Pinnock: Journey Towards Renewal*, is excellent regarding biographical and developmental details. What I am attempting to do instead is to offer an outline of Clark Pinnock's theology by examining six main themes found therein: God,

13. Pinnock, "Relational Theology," 1.

Revelation, Creation, Salvation, Church, and Hope. Certainly, this is by no means a comprehensive list, considering many other subjects might have been selected as a way of discovering his overall contribution; however, I selected these because I sense that these themes are at the heart of Pinnock's work, and I contend that in them lies Pinnock's overall contribution. My personal anticipation is that readers will be given a fairer representation of Pinnock's overall content and direction in theology. Ultimately though, I hope this volume will encourage people to read his work themselves, on its own terms, and not through the lens of secondary sources.

Further, as will become clear, this book is intentional in its prioritizing of the "later Pinnock," at the expense of the "early Pinnock." Since Pinnock's views evolved over time (as Callen documents remarkably well), I recognize that such an ambiguous distinction is difficult to make and maintain. However, such a distinction is necessary in supporting my purpose in writing. I aim *not* to chart out Pinnock's theological development, but rather, to summarize and present what Pinnock's theology came to be, in its fully bloomed state. Thus, my engagement with Pinnock's work is limited to those sources that seem to follow from his "paradigm shift" that began unfolding in the 1970s.[14]

WHY STUDY PINNOCK?

In my estimation, Clark Pinnock's theology has, in some circles, been reduced to an internal debate within Evangelical theology surrounding what has come to be known as "open theism." Though Pinnock spent a great deal of energy promoting the tenets of the open view of God—which we will discuss in detail (see chapter 1 and chapter 3, especially)[15]—I do not think that his theology should

14. Pinnock, "Response to Daniel Strange and Amos Yong," 352. Writing in 2000, Daniel Strange organizes Pinnock's life and work in three distinct phases: (1) Up to 1970, (2) 1970 to 1986, (3) 1986 to 2000. One might say that within such a paradigm, I am seeking to summarize the last two phases, though emphasizing the third and highlighting those sources within the second that remained consistent into the third. See Strange, "Biographical Essay," 1–20.

15. Rather than looking at Pinnock's "open view of God" as a whole, we

not be reduced to it, nor should it be stuck within the confines of tired stereotypes and overly simplistic summaries. In my opinion, there is much to be gleaned from both the *approach* and the *content* of Pinnock's theology that has yet to be fully appreciated by other scholars of his work/the scholarly world at large.

Relevant here is Rowan Williams's discussion of a threefold theology styles, which he refers to as *celebratory*, *communicative*, and *critical*.[16] According to Williams, celebratory theology places doctrinal language of the tradition in its best light. Communicative theology, on the other hand, moves beyond celebratory theology by establishing doctrines within new settings and expressions. The last style—critical—rather than speaking *for* the tradition, like celebratory and communicative theology, this form of theology seeks to also speak *to* the tradition. Though all three styles of theology serve various purposes, in my estimation, all three forms ought to be normed within theological discourse; however, the final category—critical or constructive theology—is perhaps the most ignored style within Evangelical scholarship.

And yet, as an Evangelical, Pinnock demonstrated an intuitive ability in write in all three styles, while focusing especially on critical/constructive theology. To be sure, at times Pinnock spoke *for* the Evangelical tradition from within it—both for the sake of those within it and those beyond it (celebratory and communicative); yet, he also invited others beyond the Evangelical tradition to speak *to* it, and from within the tradition, he sometimes joined in agreement with those who have spoken from beyond it (critical/constructive). As becomes clear in reading Pinnock, his aim was both to celebrate and communicate Evangelical theology, while also speaking critically to it in service of maturating it in its ecumenical potential. If allowed and appropriated, Pinnock's theology, has the potential to help contemporary theologians discover the value of

will be looking at the various components that make up his open view within the context of Pinnock's major theological themes. In other words, I will not dedicate a particular section of the book to Pinnock's open view, but instead, will discuss the various pieces that make up Pinnock's version of open theism as they inform and relate to the six major themes we will be addressing.

16. Williams, *On Christian Theology*, xiii.

critical/constructive theology. In his own words Pinnock says, "as for my contribution to evangelical theology, such as it is, I see it in constructive not deconstructive terms."[17] Thus, Pinnock's approach to theology—in my estimation—can aid in keeping Evangelicals from theological sectarianism.

As I mentioned earlier, I also hold the view that much of the content of Pinnock's theology is still relevant to the ongoing contemporary theological conversation. However, since my book aims, above all, to summarize the content of Pinnock's theology in an altogether fair manner, I will refrain from offering my own critical/constructive thoughts. In doing so, I hope the book will become both usable and profitable for both longtime fans as well as critics of Pinnock, while also offering first time readers of Pinnock a (somewhat) neutral ground from which to read him. Thus, by its very nature, this book invites the reader to decide for themselves what elements of Pinnock's thought are worth recovering and what elements are not.

As will become clear, Pinnock does not fit neatly within any established paradigms. Speaking of his own journey as a theologian Pinnock states,

> Not only am I not often listened to, I am also made to feel stranded theologically: being too much of a free thinker to be accepted by the Evangelical establishment and too much a conservative to be accepted by the liberal mainline. Sometimes I do not know where I belong. But I am not discouraged by this because, being a creature of hope, I can imagine a future where Evangelicals and liberals mature and come around to more sensible middle positions. I will not object to some views of mine being accepted belatedly if not now.[18]

Almost continually, Pinnock has been criticized by both theological "conservatives" and theological "liberals," sometimes nearly at the same time! Some scholars consider Pinnock to have gone too far, while others consider Pinnock to have not gone nearly far enough. Therefore, Pinnock has been reprehended from both

17. Pinnock, "Afterword," 269.

18. Pinnock, "Foreword," xvi.

sides of the proverbial aisle, as I will note throughout what follows. As such, one will have a hard time finding "Pinnockians" in the theological realm, for he does not fit neatly within any singular taxonomy. Still, whether one agrees with Pinnock wholesale or not, many have found his work to be quite stimulating. Certainly, I have.

Therefore, in providing such a volume, I wish others to be equally stimulated and inspired by Pinnock's thought. At the very least, however, I hope that the reader is stirred not only by Pinnock's theology, but by his faithfulness to Christ that is so unabashedly discerned as one reads him.[19] Therefore, as we begin to explore Pinnock's theology, it is worth sharing some of his final reflections on his own life here:

> As I look back upon my life, I am not happy with everything that I see. Nevertheless, I am (paradoxically) grateful for all that has happened, both good and bad, because God has always been with me. Everything that has happened in my life (and in the lives of all of us) has contributed to bringing us to the place where we now stand, and we should respond to the mercies of God with thankful hearts. Of course, there are things in my life that I am happy about and things which I wish had not happened, but I remember the whole story with gratitude. Just as St. Peter's denials of our Lord did not paralyze him, but once forgiven, became a source of fresh commitment, so I trust that my failures can be redeemed and that I can be an inspiration to others. Even if some of my ideas do not prove finally convincing, maybe my life as a theologian before God will nonetheless encourage and edify.[20]

With those words in mind, let us begin by exploring Pinnock's vision of a "God who is boundless love."[21]

19. Around the time of Pinnock's death, John Christopher Thomas dedicated an editorial to Pinnock in the *Journal of Pentecostal Theology*, given his frequent contributions and discussions within it. In his editorial, Thomas speaks not only to Pinnock's scholarship, but to his "remarkable nature and character" and humble and gracious spirit. Perhaps most striking is Thomas' statement that "Clark's humility and love of the Lord were evident." See Thomas, "Editorial," 1–3.

20. Pinnock, "Afterword," 269.

21. Pinnock, *Wideness to God's Mercy*, 101.

1

God: Communion of Love

WHO IS GOD? IN Pinnock's mind, how one responds to this question determines not only one's trajectory in theology, but one's direction in all of life. Frequently, people who have rejected God have confused faulty conceptions of God with God himself. In his own words, Pinnock says, "When they speak about the God whom they reject, I see little resemblance to the God of the Bible, though I do see a resemblance of the God of conventional theism."[1] As he sees it, classical Christian conceptions of God have failed to do justice to the God who has revealed himself in Jesus Christ. One of the chief tasks of the contemporary theologian, then, is to help provide a clear vision of God's beauty revealed in the gospel. Consequently, Pinnock sets out to show that rather than an all-determining, controlling, and detached monarch, God is rather a relational, cooperative, and loving parent, who has chosen to be genuinely related to his world. Though sovereign and holy, God has allowed himself to be conditioned by creatures and touched by the world's suffering, revealing that God—existing as Father, Son, and Spirit—is a "community of love and mutuality."[2] Therefore, Pinnock's doctrine

1. Pinnock, *Most Moved Mover*, 2.

2. Pinnock, *Flame of Love*, 29.

of God envisions "God as a dynamic and loving triune being who wants to have meaningful interaction with us."[3]

"A THEOLOGY OF LOVE"

Considering that love is the essence of God's being, love is not merely something God decides to do, but rather it "is what characterizes God essentially—as a dynamic livingness, a divine circling and relating."[4] Therefore, when we speak of God's love, we must recognize that it is more than an attribute—love is his very nature (1 John 4:8). Pinnock's doctrine of God is "an open view of God,"[5] which at its heart is a "theology of love."[6] That is, Pinnock's theology is grounded in and oriented toward the claim that God *is* love.

Pinnock holds that God's loving nature must intimate that God is unquestionably involved within the lives of those he loves. Since loving relationships "cannot be thought of in static terms because they are intrinsically dynamic," Pinnock suggests that God is "affected by the objects of his love and made vulnerable by them."[7] Conventional theism, Pinnock thinks, fails in this regard. Pinnock insists that classical theism struggles making sense of God as "loving, waiting, longing, repenting, and even failing."[8] Yes—"even failing." As we see in the biblical witness, God does not always get his way. Jesus' weeping over the city of Jerusalem's rejection (Matt 23:37), for instance, displays God's willingness to be subject to humanity's rejection. He is not always successful in wooing his lover. God could have created a world in which he would always "win," but since he created out of love and thereby endowed his creation

3. Pinnock and Brow, *Unbounded Love*, 10.

4. Pinnock and Brow, *Unbounded Love*, 45.

5. As I mentioned in the Introduction, we will be looking at the various tenets and components that make up Pinnock's open view of God, in chapters 1 and 3 especially. However, rather than looking at all the various components together—as has typically been done—we will be looking at these components within the context of Pinnock's major theological themes.

6. Pinnock, *Most Moved Mover*, 82.

7. Pinnock, *Most Moved Mover*, 82.

8. Pinnock, *Most Moved Mover*, 82.

with freedom, he has made himself subject to disappointment and suffering. That is to say that Pinnock pays great attention to "the personal nature of God's relationality."[9]

Yet, what about God's wrath? Does making God's love central curtail such a category? In Pinnock's words:

> Making love central does not make wrath unreal. . . . Rather, wrath signals that God is not indifferent to our human response. He is a jealous God and cares about what we do with what he gives. This is a "holy" love that claims us so seriously that it does not tolerate spiritual adultery. It is a love that wants to change us and not leave us the same. When we refuse love's offer, God manifests himself to us in another way—as wrath. God becomes wrathful because he loves us. God would not become angry if he was not loving.[10]

This suggests that wrath "arises out of the pathos of love."[11] God *is* love—God is not wrath. Wrath, in other words, does not belong to God's nature. Thus, love and wrath are not on "equal footing" within the life of God. Rather, God becomes wrathful because of his love. One (wrath), then, is derived from and in service of the other (love).

But let us return to where we started. In reflecting upon the biblical expression "God is love" (1 John 4:8), Pinnock assumes that this refers to God's inner life. What might, then, this imply about God? Not using Pinnock's words, one could say that a God who is everlastingly love by nature cannot be a unitarian God. Such a God would require creation for self-actualization, for instance. On Pinnock's account, other monotheistic faiths have the problem of a "lonely God," but not Christianity.[12] The Christian God, then, "is not a featureless monad, isolated and motionless, but a dynamic

9. Pinnock, "Divine Relationality," 5.

10. Pinnock, *Most Moved Mover*, 82–83.

11. Pinnock, *Most Moved Mover*, 83.

12. Pinnock, *Most Moved Mover*, 83.

event of actions and personal relationality."[13] Therefore, God is satisfied within his own trinitarian life of love.

Pinnock also interprets Jesus' statement, "As the Father has loved me, so I have loved you" (John 15:9) to reference the triune love that flows between the persons of the Godhead.[14] Like Jürgen Moltmann, Colin Gunton, and other theologians,[15] Pinnock adopts a social model of the Trinity, for which he names the twelfth century theologian Richard St. Victor as an early proponent.[16] Thus, when formulating a trinitarian model, Pinnock moves from plurality to unity. Father, Son, and Spirit exist in a dynamic of love. The divine unity, then, lies in "the relationality of Persons, and the relationality is the nature of the unity."[17] He is careful to evade tritheism by holding that the Trinity is a "society of persons united by a common divinity."[18]

Along with other contemporary theologians, Pinnock repudiates divine simplicity.[19] As he puts it, "'Simplicity' is . . . one of the most alien of the Greek-influenced attributes of God."[20] In its place, he seeks to recover the Cappadocian insight that God is essentially complex.[21] The Cappadocian Fathers believed that it is the relatedness of the identities that make up God. Therefore, in Pinnock's reading of Christian history, "the early patristics were relational

13. Pinnock, *Flame of Love*, 42.

14. Pinnock, *Flame of Love*, 30.

15. See Moltmann, *Trinity and the Kingdom*; Gunton, *Promise of Trinitarian Theology*.

16. Pinnock, *Flame of Love*, 33.

17. Pinnock, *Flame of Love*, 30.

18. Pinnock, *Flame of Love*, 35.

19. Divine simplicity states God does not exist in parts but is totally unified, with no distinct attributes, and whose existence is synonymous with God's essence.

20. Pinnock, *Most Moved Mover*, 84.

21. Like Robert Jenson, Pinnock holds that prior to Augustine, God was thought to be essentially related to his creation. As Jenson states, "Augustine rejected the Cappadocian doctrine for the sake of his simplicity axiom." See Jenson, *Triune Identity*, 119; Jenson, *Systematic Theology*, 110–19.

theists."[22] Thus, relationality is not foreign to the Christian tradition, which renders the exchange of substance ontology for relational ontology easier in Pinnock's mind. He believes theology needs a robust "vision of the triune God as an event of open, dynamic, loving relations."[23] This understanding of the Trinity leads Pinnock to claim that "there is only one God, but this one God is not solitary but a loving communion that is distinguished by overflowing love."[24] God is not undifferentiated unity. The Trinity is not drawn from God's essence. Rather, the Trinity *is* God's loving essence. One cannot move outside the relations of Father, Son, and Spirit to an essence that anticipates them—for there is no such essence. Pinnock, thus, agrees with John Zizioulas that "the substance of God, 'God,' has no ontological content, no true being, apart from communion."[25] Consequently, trinitarian relations compose the being of God.

Father

We know God as Father because of Jesus, whom the biblical writ and tradition both depict as his "Son." The revelation of God as Father, in Pinnock's estimation, "belongs to revelation that originated not in time but in eternity."[26] Therefore, God-the-Father language cannot be simply interchanged with God-the-Parent or God-the-Mother language.[27] While Pinnock acknowledges that there are maternal images of God to be found in Scripture, he does not think female imagery should supplant the originative guiding symbol of God's Fatherhood.[28] Even though Pinnock insists upon the primacy of God-the-Father language, he does not think that this should ever lead to identifying God as male, since God is "beyond gender."[29]

22. Pinnock, "Divine Relationality," 16–17.

23. Pinnock, *Flame of Love*, 42.

24. Pinnock, *Flame of Love*, 31.

25. Zizioulas, *Being as Communion*, 17.

26. Pinnock and Brown, *Theological Crossfire*, 77.

27. Pinnock and Brown, *Theological Crossfire*, 76–77.

28. Pinnock and Brown, *Theological Crossfire*, 77.

29. Pinnock and Brow, *Unbounded Love*, 31.

The truth is that masculinity and femininity both find their origin in God, and thus God "ministers to us in the capacity of both parents."[30]

Throughout his work, Pinnock wishes to show that Jesus reveals the Father *not* as "a patriarchal figure who is fond of domination," but rather as one "who upends power and calls for mutual relationships."[31] While some make "king" the key metaphor for God, emphasizing God as causal, others lift the metaphor of "judge" to preeminence, underscoring God as an enactor of justice. However, Pinnock consistently accentuates the metaphor of God as a divine "Father." In Pinnock's mind, we cannot conceive of God as Father in any way that is contrary to Jesus' portrayal of God as the father in the story of the prodigal son (Luke 15:11–32). Pinnock perceives Jesus' metaphor of the Father within this parable as communicating that God "loves us unconditionally."[32] For Pinnock, this illustration of the Father underscores God's loving nature, and consequently, he declares that it ought to be "the central image" which "controls the meaning of the other metaphors" found in Scripture.[33]

Jesus

Overall, Pinnock's theology is Christocentric: "Christology is the hinge on which the Christian system turns. Although all doctrines relate to one another, there is a sense in which Christology is the focal point of [all] Christian truth."[34] Like other Evangelical theologians, Pinnock wants to underline the centrality of Christ in all of Christian theology. However, unlike many Evangelical theologians, Pinnock confronts "Hellenistic developments" within classical christological formulations. When it comes to Christology, in

30. Pinnock and Brow, *Unbounded Love*, 53.
31. Pinnock and Brow, *Unbounded Love*, 32.
32. Pinnock and Brow, *Unbounded Love*, 29.
33. Pinnock and Brow, *Unbounded Love*, 29.
34. Pinnock and Brown, *Theological Crossfire*, 139.

Pinnock's own words, "there are difficulties that Evangelicals need to respond to."[35]

In Pinnock's conceptions, most scholars have preferred to interpret the event of Jesus Christ in terms of the divine Logos, as spirit, taking on flesh. Though Logos Christology is biblically grounded, it has unfortunately "eclipsed other possibilities, including Spirit Christology."[36] The heresy deemed "adoptionism" by its critics necessitated the development of Logos Christology within the Christian tradition, but since "we are not driven by these factors now," Pinnock calls for theologians to address the "one-sidedness in our thinking."[37] To be sure, he does not call for a rejection of Logos Christology, but rather questions its dominance over other models, such as Spirit Christology.

Steven Studebaker has helpfully noted that while some scholars have suggested substituting Spirit Christology for Logos Christology due to their nontraditional trinitarian perspective, this is not the case for Pinnock.[38] Rather, as we should expect from Pinnock, his effort to offer a Spirit Christology that is complementary to Logos Christology stems from his desire to recover biblical perspectives that have been traditionally overlooked. Different models, for instance, are used by different biblical witnesses. As he puts it, "Christology of the New Testament is complex not simple."[39] Pinnock believes that if we take a fresh look at the synoptic gospel's portrayal of Jesus, we will discover how often Jesus relates to the Spirit in significant moments throughout his life. For example, Jesus was anointed by the Spirit in Mary's womb (Matt 1:18). As he maturated in youth, the Spirit blessed him with grace and wisdom (Luke 2:52). According to the biblical witness, the Spirit fell upon

35. Pinnock and Brown, *Theological Crossfire*, 145.

36. Pinnock, *Flame of Love*, 80. By Logos Christology Pinnock means the perspective that emerges as a result of viewing the event of Jesus Christ in terms of the divine Logos becoming flesh, based on John's gospel. Spirit Christology, in contrast, refers to viewing Christ from the standpoint of the Spirit, which in Pinnock's view, is how the Synoptic gospels writers portrayed Jesus.

37. Pinnock, *Flame of Love*, 80.

38. Studebaker, "Integrating Pneumatology," 7.

39. Pinnock and Brown, *Theological Crossfire*, 145.

Jesus in power at his baptism (Matt 3:16). The Spirit thereafter led him into the wilderness, where he was tested (Matt 4:1). Jesus was further anointed by the Spirit for his ministry (Luke 4:18), which led him to declare: "It is by the Spirit of God that I cast out demons" (Matt 12:28).

Pinnock imagines this reveals that Jesus "was the Son of God who nevertheless emptied himself to live in solidarity with others, as dependent on the Spirit as any of them."[40] The eternal Son became "weak, powerless and dependent on the Spirit."[41] As such, by the Spirit, Jesus was conceived, anointed, empowered, directed, commissioned, and resurrected. As one might discern, Pinnock appreciates the contributions of kenotic Christology.[42] Pinnock, then, is able to speak of the "dependence" of Christ upon the Spirit. According to his rendering, the eternal Son surrendered the independent use of his divine attributes in the incarnation, necessitating his reliance upon the Spirit.[43] Therefore, rather than accentuating the hypostatic union, Pinnock asserts that the Spirit's anointing is what made Jesus the "Christ." Jesus' sinlessness, too, was due to his perfect relation to the Spirit, rather than his own ontological constitution as deity. Here Pinnock agrees with Vladmir Lossky's statement: "Christ never, or almost never, asserts his divinity."[44]As Pinnock sees it:

> It is important to recognize that Jesus was dependent on the Spirit. He had to rely on the Spirit's resources to

40. Pinnock, *Flame of Love*, 85.

41. Pinnock, *Flame of Love*, 81.

42. In theology, *kenosis* refers to the self-emptying of Christ in the incarnation (Phil 2:7–11). In the nineteenth century, certain theologians utilized the concept of *kenosis* within Christology to argue that the self-emptying of Christ in the incarnation involved the setting aside of certain divine attributes. In Pinnock's words, "kenotic theory, is, I think, the most important fresh contribution to Christology since early centuries" since it "raises the intelligibility of orthodoxy and robs its critics of much of their ammunition against the doctrine of the incarnation." See Pinnock and Brown, *Theological Crossfire*, 146–47. Further, as we will find out, when Pinnock refers to *kenosis*, he is referring to God's self-limitations.

43. Pinnock, *Flame of Love*, 88.

44. Lossky, *Dogmatic Theology*, 117.

> overcome temptation. He was weak and human and did not know the life of undiminished deity. He suffered real attack in the temptations and was not play-acting. It was not through confidence in his own power that he put himself at risk. Victory over temptation was not achieved in his own strength.[45]

It is important to be clear on this point: Pinnock holds that Jesus was *not* simply a man endowed with the Spirit.[46] Rather, his Spirit Christology aims to enrich Logos Christology by giving greater attention to the position of the Spirit in Christ. In his mind, this "gives better recognition to the missions of both the Son and the Spirit" by neither exaggerating nor diminishing "the role of either Person."[47] So then, when Pinnock speaks of Spirit Christology he does so "in an orthodox way that preserves the trinitarian distinctions."[48] Therefore, as one commentator has stated, "Pinnock's Spirit-Christology connects *kenosis* Christology to Logos Christology."[49]

Spirit

It has been said that Pinnock's *Flame of Love* "may be the most significant pneumatological work by a contemporary evangelical."[50] While the title of this work may seem to suggest that Pinnock has provided a doctrine of the third person of the Trinity, he has instead produced a one-volume systematic theology with the Holy Spirit as its central, integrative motif. As one reads the work, it becomes clear that Pinnock believes that of all doctrines, "pneumatology is most promising of fresh discoveries, because it has

45. Pinnock, *Flame of Love*, 88.

46. In other words, Pinnock's Spirit Christology does not resemble those of Geoffrey Lamp and John Hick, for example.

47. Pinnock, *Flame of Love*, 92.

48. Pinnock, *Flame of Love*, 92.

49. Bryant, *Spirit Christology*, 32.

50. Kärkkäinen, *Holy Spirit*, 91.

suffered neglect relative to other topics of theology."[51] Taken as a whole, one might consider his developed theology as marked by a pneumatological-Christocentricism.

Pinnock notes that while in one sense God's nature is Spirit, the *Holy Spirit* refers to the third person in the divine community. Even though Pinnock follows Augustine's claim that the Spirit is the love that bonds the Father and Son, he is quick to note that this image falls short of ascribing personality to the Spirit. Within this framework, the Spirit is too easily reduced to merely fostering the "environment of love," without it being understood that the Spirit is sharing and participating in it.[52] Since the Spirit is revealed nonexclusively—unlike the Father and Son whose names bespeak particularity and relationality—the Holy Spirit could be understood as an "it" rather than a divine person. But because the Spirit is a personal, divine agent, Pinnock insists that our language must promote the Spirit's personhood.

As we have seen, Pinnock resists using feminine language for the Father and Son "for obvious reasons."[53] However, when it comes to the person of the Spirit, Pinnock believes that feminine language is completely appropriate. Since God is not gendered, Pinnock considers the use of either personal pronouns "he" or "she" as permissible when speaking of the Spirit. Considering the many facets of the Spirit's work that appear to be feminine (such as life-giving, birthing, comforting, etc.), he recommends using the personal pronoun "she" for the Spirit.[54] In doing so, Pinnock believes it can help affirm that both men and women are equally made in the image of God, while also, in his words, enriching "religious experience by allowing us to access the Spirit's feminine side."[55]

51. Pinnock, "Role of the Spirit in Creation," 47.

52. Pinnock, *Flame of Love*, 40.

53. Pinnock, "Role of the Spirit in Creation," 48.

54. Pinnock, "Role of the Spirit in Creation," 48.

55. Pinnock, "Role of the Spirit in Creation," 48. Pinnock mentions InterVarsity Press advised against using the feminine pronoun for the Spirit in *Flame of Love*. Pinnock surmises that "there must have been a calculation as to which group among its readers is larger—the group wanting to make moves toward greater inclusion or the group nervous about making concessions to

"THE METAPHYSICS OF LOVE"

"Having a vision of reality helps one navigate the world because it offers categories to help formulate doctrine and holds promise for apologetic gain."[56] These words demonstrate that theology must inevitably engage in metaphysics for Pinnock.[57] Though some theologians have sought to abandon metaphysics altogether, Pinnock recognizes that Christian beliefs implicitly involve metaphysical claims. Notions such as creation, miracles, revelation, and God, for instance, all bear implications about the construction of reality. In Pinnock's mind, then, the question is not *if* one's theology is influenced by philosophical categories, but *how* one's theology is influenced by them. Or to say the same thing another way, "we all do metaphysics—the challenge is whether the metaphysics we do is of the right kind."[58]

On Pinnock's account, the early theologians were influenced by Hellenistic philosophy. As a result, God was thought to be an "infinite, unbounded ocean of being and as a subsistent Being in which all beings share, one who is infinitely and qualitatively different than the world."[59] Though he considers the early engagement with Hellenistic philosophy and its substance metaphysics as an understandable component of the development of Christian theology, he believes that there are better contemporary resources available that can assist theology in capturing the biblical portrait of God. In other words, Pinnock understands that "not every philosophical

any kind of feminism." Considering this, in *Flame of Love*, Pinnock admits that "something in me wants to use the feminine pronoun" (17) but in the end decides to use the masculine pronoun, apparently following the publisher's recommendation. However, the following year (1997), Pinnock published a journal article making an argument for why he believes using the feminine pronoun "she" for the Spirit is the better of the two options. See Pinnock, *Flame of Love*, 15–17; Pinnock, "Role of the Spirit in Creation," 48.

56. Pinnock, *Most Moved Mover*, 114.

57. Metaphysics is the philosophical study of ultimate reality beyond the physical. It is related to questions concerning what establishes something as "real" or as having "being."

58. Pinnock, *Most Moved Mover*, 116.

59. Pinnock, *Most Moved Mover*, 116–17.

resource is equally valid for theology."[60] He considers dynamic, relational categories—for instance—to better fit conceptually the biblical data than the traditional static, non-relational ones.

Pinnock admits that process philosophy,[61] with its emphasis upon God's dynamic interaction with the world, has helpfully contributed philosophical resources that Christian doctrine ought to consider. Although Pinnock appreciates some components of *process philosophy*, he is noticeably vocal in his criticisms of *process theology*. He states, for example, "When I read process theologians, I realize two things: first that we need a theism which is more dynamic than the traditional view, and second that we need a God who is more deserving of that title (God) than Whitehead's godling is."[62] Pinnock urges Christian theologians to consider the strengths of modern philosophical systems, without becoming overly reliant upon them. As he sees it, although Christian theologians "can adapt a metaphysics," they should not "adopt one."[63] In Pinnock's logic, the weaknesses of both classical and process theisms are their over-reliance upon metaphysical systems. Therefore, in response to the one-sidedness of both, Pinnock sets out to construct a model of God which "keeps a proper balance between transcendence and immanence and makes such adjustments in our thinking about God as will serve the dynamic biblical presentation in a faithful way."[64]

God and Creation

What, then, might we say regarding God's relationship to creation? According to Pinnock, we need a doctrine of God that envisions

60. Pinnock, *Most Moved Mover*, 117.

61. Process theology is a twentieth century movement based on the philosophy of Alfred North Whitehead that emphasizes God as intrinsically entangled in the process of the world. Major proponents include Charles Hartshorne and John B. Cobb Jr.

62. Pinnock, "Between Classical and Process Theism," 325. Pinnock is, of course, referring to the notable twentieth century process philosopher Alfred North Whitehead.

63. Cobb and Pinnock, *Searching for an Adequate God*, xi.

64. Pinnock, "Between Classical and Process Theism," 312–13.

"God as transcendent over the world and yet existing in an open and mutually affecting relationship with the world."[65] Therefore, his proposal aims to maintain mutuality and reciprocity within the framework of divine transcendence. To begin, Pinnock affirms that God creates the world out of nothing. Thus, "everything depends on God for its existence."[66] Against classical theism, though, Pinnock argues that God is dynamic rather than static, but against process theology, he states that God is Lord of the cosmos and not a finite god. Therefore, as he puts it, "I think it would be fair to say that my proposal constitutes a *via media*."[67] Yet, what does this proposal look like?

In Pinnock's rendering, God did not need to create, since he exists in "trinitarian fullness."[68] Therefore, God's self-sufficiency implies that creation happens by grace, not by necessity. God decided to create out of love so that creation could freely and voluntarily participate in his own life of love. Thus, the all-powerful God has chosen to limit his power to make room for a free creation. This kenotic act of "self-limitation" is not necessary but voluntary. Because God desires to be "involved in creation and to give the creature some 'say so' in the flow of history," he restricts the full use of his power.[69] As Pinnock articulates it, this is not a "renunciation of ontological powers but a way of exercising those very powers in love."[70]

Therefore, since God endowed his creation with freedom, "creation was also an act of self-limitation, not of self-expansion."[71] Because God is omnipotent, he could control all things. However,

65. Pinnock, "Between Classical and Process Theism," 321.

66. Pinnock, "Systematic Theology," 109.

67. Pinnock, "Between Classical and Process Theism," 321.

68. Pinnock, *Flame of Love*, 44.

69. Pinnock, "Constrained by Love," 150. Though Pinnock, at times, talks about God being "constrained," as I read him, I believe he is actually talking about being "restrained." In other words, Pinnock does not believe God is necessarily constrained by outside forces, but rather has chosen only to be constrained by his own self-restraint.

70. Pinnock, "Constrained by Love," 150.

71. Pinnock, *Most Moved Mover*, 31.

God has chosen to self-limit/self-restrain his power in relation to creation in order to make room for free creatures.[72] This implies that "God is sovereign over his own sovereignty."[73] Ontologically speaking, Pinnock states that God is transcendent over the world, while also indwelling it. God affects the world, while also allowing it to affect him. Though there is more to be said regarding Pinnock's formulation of the God-world relationship (see chapter 3), for now it is sufficient to point out that Pinnock seeks to affirm God's transcendence *over* creation, while simultaneously arguing for God's immanence *within* creation.

Faithfulness and Contingency

If one is going to promote a personal model of God—which Pinnock does in fact—one must also revise how one talks about the attributes of God. And this is exactly what Pinnock achieves. He believes that "if we are to bring the relationality dimension into theology,"[74] we must be prepared to engage in a "metaphysical revolution."[75] He notes that there has been a tendency within the Christian tradition to place God as "far away from and as high over us as possible."[76] Further, he states that the typical categories of infinity, immutability, atemporality, impassibility, simplicity, omnipotence, omniscience, etc. give the impression that God is "far away, aloof, and cold."[77] In Pinnock's mind, "assumptions about what is proper for the divine nature to be like can make it difficult for us to take seriously what God's nature is like as revealed in the gospel."[78]

When it comes to immutability, for instance, Pinnock states that the category needs to "focus on the faithfulness of God as a

72. This means that when Pinnock speaks of *kenosis*, he is referring to God's self-limitations.

73. Pinnock, "Clark Pinnock's Response to Part 1," 84.

74. Pinnock, "Divine Relationality," 18.

75. Pinnock, *Most Moved Mover*, 27.

76. Pinnock, "Clark Pinnock's Response to Part 2," 147.

77. Pinnock, "Clark Pinnock's Response to Part 2," 147–48.

78. Pinnock and Brow, *Unbounded Love*, 31.

relational, personal being" rather than on God's static unchangeability.[79] Yes, God is unchanging in nature and essence—God is not a contingent being. Yet, Pinnock thinks the category of immutability has often overlooked how God changes in his experiences, knowledge, and actions.[80] Even though God is "immutable in essence," in other respects, God does change.[81] His nature is constant, but since he willingly decides to allow the world to affect him and his experiences, Pinnock thinks a better term for the concept of immutability is "changeable faithfulness."[82] This implies that God is completely reliable and true, while simultaneously being "flexible in his dealings and able to change course, as circumstances require."[83]

Pinnock exclaims that he is often perplexed by Evangelicals who make much out of their presumed devotion to Scripture, while at the same time, uncritically swallowing "the pagan legacy of the absolute immutability of God."[84] He thinks that biblical categories such as suffering, repentance, and temporality should lead one to see God as lively not apathetic. The Bible speaks of God as one whose nature does not change, but his relationships and actions often do. To put it another way, though God himself is not contingent, "there is contingency in God's experiences of the world."[85] On this theme, Pinnock's thought resembles the American philosopher and theologian Nicholas Wolterstorff, who writes:

> God's ontological immutability (the strong sense) is not part of the explicit teaching of the biblical writers. What the biblical writers teach is that God is faithful and

79. Pinnock, "Systematic Theology," 117.

80. Pinnock, "Systematic Theology,"118.

81. Pinnock, "Systematic Theology,"117–18. Perhaps it is important to note that when Pinnock speaks of God changing, he is expressing a uniquely divine kind of changeability. He is not implying that God is a contingent being, but rather that God has bound himself up experientially with his creation.

82. Pinnock, *Most Moved Mover*, 85.

83. Pinnock, *Most Moved Mover*, 85.

84. Pinnock, "Clark Pinnock's Response to Part 2," 148. Pinnock shares that he finds it ironic when some Evangelicals question his orthodoxy on this point, when "my only slip has been to prefer the Bible to Plato."

85. Pinnock, *Most Moved Mover*, 86.

> without beginning or end, not that none of his aspects is temporal (the weak sense). The theological tradition of God's ontological immutability has no explicit biblical foundations.[86]

Pinnock assumes that affirming God's "changeable faithfulness" does not in any way make God fickle. God's responsiveness does not undermine God's trustworthiness. On Pinnock's reading, Scripture is clear that God is "faithful to the creation project and has committed himself to redeem it."[87] Therefore, God's own "resourcefulness, wisdom, and patience can guarantee the end of history."[88] Hence, we can be confident in the ultimate victory of God, due to his resourcefulness, wisdom, and faithfulness. Despite the presence of obstacles along the way, God will prevail in the end.

Because of God's relationship with his creation, though, God does not always get his way. God is love, which suggests that he is involved with the world and is affected by creatures. His will can be frustrated. This, of course, challenges the traditional view of the impassibility of God.[89] But Pinnock believes that God's loving nature rules out any notion that God would lack vulnerability: "How can God love us and experience nothing? How does God avoid suffering if he is intimately involved with the world?"[90] On Pinnock's account, God cannot both be loving and indifferent. Additionally, impassibility seems to undermine the experienced suffering and death of the Jesus. Due to Christ, "divine suffering lies at the heart of the Christian faith."[91] Scripture portrays a God who suffers *because of* his people, *for* his people, and *with* his people. Here he resembles Dietrich Bonhoeffer, who notes that: "The Bible directs man to God's powerlessness and suffering—only a suffering God can help."[92] According to Pinnock, the suffering or pathos of God is

86. Wolterstorff, "God Everlasting," 202.
87. Pinnock, *Most Moved Mover*, 138.
88. Pinnock, *Most Moved Mover*, 139.
89. Pinnock, *Most Moved Mover*, 88.
90. Pinnock, *Most Moved Mover*, 90.
91. Pinnock, *Most Moved Mover*, 89.
92. Bonhoeffer, *Letters and Papers from Prison*, 188.

a strong theme throughout the biblical canon: "God's love, wrath, jealousy and suffering are all prominent."[93]

Pinnock observes, though, that God does not experience *pathos* the same way his creatures do:

> At the same time, impassibility is a subtle idea with a grain of truth. We have to distinguish ways in which God can suffer from ways in which God cannot suffer. God is beyond certain modes of suffering, just as he is beyond certain modes of change. We could say that God is impassible in nature but passible in his experience of the world. Change occurs in the world and affects God when he becomes aware of it. When that change involves innocent suffering (for example), God responds tenderly to it.[94]

In short, though Pinnock asserts that God is passible, he does not assume that God is passible in the same way we are. However, Pinnock wants to understand God's attributes based on God's own self-disclosure, rather than on how Hellenistic philosophy has sought to understand them.

God's Eternity

Because God is personal, Pinnock affirms that God must also be temporal and inside, not outside, of time. Pinnock puts it this way: "whatever God's eternity is like, it includes the possibility of time and the capacity to relate to us within time."[95] Hence, it is not surprising that Pinnock regards the classical Christian claim that God is timeless as problematic. In his view, God's eternity "does not cancel or annihilate time but stands in a positive relation to it, which is for us not against us."[96]

Pinnock thinks that one of the major distinctions between Christianity and Hellenism is their conflicting interpretations of

93. Pinnock, "Systematic Theology," 118.

94. Pinnock, "Systematic Theology," 119.

95. Pinnock, *Most Moved Mover*, 99.

96. Pinnock, "Systematic Theology," 120.

God and time. Put another way, Pinnock believes that the God of Scripture "was eternal by his faithfulness *through* time" rather than the Greek gods' "abstraction *from* time."[97] Rather, his eternity "means that there has never been and never will be a time when God does not exist."[98] If we follow the depiction that God is essentially outside the whole order of creation, Pinnock believes this suggests that "God is essentially non-relational and uninvolved" with it.[99] As Pinnock reads Scripture, it portrays God as the Creator of space and time and as one who experiences time.

> In relation to time, God created cosmic time and relates to it as a temporal divine agent. God is at home with temporality, and his life is temporally ordered. God's temporality is strongly taught in Scripture. For example, God makes plans and carries them out. He speaks of past, present, and future. God anticipates and plans for the future, he remembers things that are past, and he addresses his people in the present.[100]

Pinnock sees God existing before creation and before creaturely time, but since his creation, he "then has related to the world within the structures of time."[101] God's life, then, is temporally ordered, at least, from the time of creation. He is not beyond the movement of time and history, looking down on the earth, but has instead decided to join in on the flow of history. This implies that "past, present and future are real to God."[102] Sure, because God is eternal, God is immune from the ravages of time, is free from our inability to remember, and so forth."[103] However, God still is with us in time, "experiencing the succession of events with us."[104] Therefore, Pinnock attempts to affirm God's transcendence over

97. Jenson, *Triune Identity*, 58.

98. Pinnock, "Systematic Theology," 121.

99. Pinnock, "Constrained by Love," 154.

100. Pinnock, "Constrained by Love," 155.

101. Pinnock, *Most Moved Mover*, 97.

102. Pinnock, "Systematic Theology," 120.

103. Pinnock, "Systematic Theology," 120.

104. Pinnock, "Systematic Theology," 120.

creaturely experience of time, but not in a way that is in isolation from the world. God's presence saturates everything he has created "such that every part of it exists in him, though his being is much more than and is not exhausted" by it.[105] Pinnock believes that in producing creation, God decided to "immerse" himself in it. This means that God does not need to work from outside the created order, since God is present in it.

Pinnock recognizes that this view of God and time may cause some to think that God is limited, but he tends to think, in opposition to such a view, that it actually heightens God's majesty and beauty. For instance, if God did not have temporal experiences, "the personal dimension of the divine life would be very hard to determine" and "history would be little more than a boring drawing out of what has already been determined."[106] Instead, by God "bringing into being a temporal creation, the nature of which is realized in its unfolding history, God has greatly honored and given significance to time."[107]

But if God is in time with us, what does this say about God's knowledge? Because Pinnock believes that God considers his creatures partners, he argues that "history is not yet completely settled but is still being actualized."[108] In Pinnock's logic, if the future is not "open," then neither God nor humanity can contribute anything to it. However, if the future is still being shaped, then our decisions are only possibilities until they are actualized. In Pinnock's words, "It makes sense to think about the future as partly settled and partly unsettled, otherwise it would be the realm of settled actualities and not open possibilities, which would undercut meaningful human life."[109] He believes that this idea makes sense of the biblical texts that speak of God being sincerely surprised and changing his mind based on new circumstances. Though such references are often ignored or explained away because the tradition has assumed that

105. Pinnock, "Constrained by Love," 155.

106. Pinnock, "Constrained by Love," 155.

107. Pinnock, "Constrained by Love," 155.

108. Pinnock, *Most Moved Mover*, 102.

109. Pinnock, *Most Moved Mover*, 137.

they cannot mean what they seem to say, Pinnock considers them to shed light on the fact that "God faces a partly unsettled future."[110]

Therefore, since the future has not been entirely established, divine omniscience—in Pinnock's view—is not synonymous with exhaustive foreknowledge of all future events,[111] but rather, denotes the fact that God knows everything that can be known. Pinnock speaks of a "kenosis of omniscience,"[112] meaning *not* that God limits his knowledge, but rather that God voluntarily chose to create a universe that is still unfolding and becoming, thus constraining his knowledge of all future events.[113]

> He knows everything that has ever existed, everything that now actually exists, everything that could possibly exist in future, and everything that he has decided to do. The details of his knowledge change as creatures act in new and free ways. This not a limitation on God as knower; it has to do with the nature of the future as partly settled and partly unsettled. God knows everything that can be known and that is perfection enough.[114]

Pinnock believes this view of the future and God's knowability inclines humanity to assume responsibility for the future.[115] He also thinks this view of omniscience is better fitted to "relational theism." As he views it, if humans are true partners and co-laborers

110. Pinnock, *Most Moved Mover*, 47.

111. Pinnock, "Systematic Theology," 121.

112. Pinnock, "Constrained by Love," 156.

113. Here I am being charitable in my reading of Pinnock. As one reads him on divine omniscience, it becomes clear he is inconsistent on this point. Often, he states that God does not know the future exhaustively because God has limited or restrained his knowledge. However, his open view of the future carries with it the understanding that God does not know some of the parts of the future that exist only as possibilities. Within this framework, God is not "self-limited" when it comes to his knowledge. Rather, he knows all that there is to know.

114. Pinnock, *Most Moved Mover*, 138.

115. Pinnock, *Most Moved Mover*, 137.

with God, there must be room for us to participate in shaping the future with God.[116]

While Pinnock recognizes that some individuals find exhaustive foreknowledge comforting, Pinnock himself finds the notion "frightening." In his mind, exhaustive foreknowledge describes a future that is inevitable and static. He also believes it paints God to be controlling and unimaginative. Ordaining everything before creation requires no wisdom or resourcefulness on God's part, for instance. However, if creation is an open project—which Pinnock believes it is—then God must be omni-wise and omni-resourceful. Pinnock says, "it is the wisdom of God that we marvel at, not abstract omniscience."[117] Even if God does not always get his way, he is ingenious, and thus will win the final victory over sin. Pinnock, in his way of stating it, says, "we can be sure that God, as a kind of master chess player, will win, but we cannot be sure exactly how the end game will play itself out."[118]

CONCLUSION

As we have seen, Pinnock seeks to find a way between classical theism and process theism. In his view, what is needed is a middle way between these two "extremes." However, because of this fact, he has often been criticized by voices on both sides. Process theologian Cobb, for instance, has noted that Pinnock, along with other freewill or open theists, prefer to affirm the Bible's anthropomorphic representations of God over and above "rational coherence of doctrine of avoiding intellectual problems."[119] Similarly, "liberal" theologian Delwin Brown finds Pinnock's doctrine of God "unsatisfactory" since he leaves open the possibility of God's intervention into

116. Pinnock, "Clark Pinnock's Response to Part 2," 151. However, Pinnock admits that "my critique of exhaustive omniscience is not a necessary part of a relational model but only a possible detail of it, so that a relational theist need not accept it." See Pinnock, "Divine Relationality," 20.

117. Pinnock, *Most Moved Mover*, 52.

118. Pinnock, *Most Moved Mover*, 52.

119. Cobb and Pinnock, "Introduction," xiii.

human affairs.[120] Nevertheless, Bruce Ware—a conservative, Evangelical Calvinist—states that Pinnock's doctrine of God with its "denial of exhaustive divine foreknowledge, has shown itself to be unacceptable as a viable, legitimate model within evangelicalism."[121]

Even considering these criticisms—among others—Pinnock admits that he "can see no other way of showing respect for the biblical presentation of God as a dynamic personal" agent.[122] In his mind, "liberals listen to modern voices too much" in shaping their view of God,[123] while conservative "paleo-Calvinists" too often "uncritically swallow" the tradition of the church, even if it means accepting unbiblical, pagan legacies.[124] As it has been demonstrated, Pinnock's theology is marked by a personal God, who is dynamically related to the world. He hopes, then, to propose a doctrine of God "lying between the two feuding protagonists" which he hopes "will outrun them both."[125]

To understand Pinnock's theological reasoning, though, we must also examine his understanding of revelation. And to that task we now turn.

120. Pinnock and Brown, *Theological Crossfire*, 78.

121. Ware, "Defining Evangelicalism's Boundaries," 212.

122. Pinnock, "Between Classical and Process Theism," 323.

123. Pinnock and Brown, *Theological Crossfire*, 96.

124. Pinnock, "Clark Pinnock's Response to Part 2," 148.

125. Pinnock, "Between Classical and Process Theism," 326.

2

Revelation: Following the Spirit

PINNOCK CONSIDERS REVELATION THE "dynamic self-disclosure of God, who makes his goodness known in the history of salvation," climaxing in the person of Jesus Christ.[1] Though Jesus is the definitive revelation of God,[2] the truth of Christ is mediated through various secondary "sources" of revelation. However, Pinnock had not always retained this position. As Barry Callen has noted, over his career, Pinnock moved from being "a fierce defender of a Reformed fundamentalistic" biblicism to an advocate of a "gentler and nuanced," revelationally rooted model of revelation, symbolized by the Wesleyan quadrilateral.[3] Over time Pinnock grew to appreciate that revelation is not self-interpreting. He came to emphasize the need for the Spirit to "lead us into all truth" (John 16:13). As we grow as hearers of the w/Word, the Spirit guides us into greater understanding over time. This suggests, for Pinnock, that development in attaining disclosed truth is always possible. What is needed, then, is humility, discernment, and interpretive approaches that can better enable us to follow the Spirit.

1. Pinnock, *Flame of Love*, 226.
2. Pinnock, *Tracking the Maze*, 163.
3. Callen, *Journey Toward Renewal*, 41.

DEFINING REVELATION

What is revelation? Before speaking positively, Pinnock seeks to define what revelation is *not*: "Revelation is neither human transformation alone nor a set of propositions on a variety of topics."[4] His dissatisfaction with liberalism's overemphasis upon experience and conservatism's insistence upon timeless propositions, leads him to avoid reducing revelation to either subjective perceptions or rationalistic principles. Instead, Pinnock seeks to construct a balanced, mediating position on the relationship between the experiential and cognitive aspects of revelation. Therefore, rather than developing a view of revelation that perhaps errs too closely on either side, Pinnock aims to construct one that is rooted in God's own self-disclosure. As Pinnock sees it, revelation is "not primarily existential impact or infallible truths," but rather "self-disclosure and interpersonal communication."[5] Said differently, revelation is an "introduction to a person."[6] As such, it includes "historical actions, verbal disclosures, and personal encounters."[7]

Though God worked within history prior to Christ, Jesus is the fullest expression of God's revelation. He is the image of the invisible God (John 1:18; Col 1:15). In Jesus, "God has drawn back the veil of mystery and disclosed a portion of who he is."[8] This suggests that revelation maintains a relational center.[9] His conception of revelation as *self*-revelation also implies that as we grow into Christ, we are able to mature into greater comprehension of truth. Though revelation itself does not grow, "our understanding of it may be refined and amplified through action and reflection."[10] This development remains personally and individually grounded since the Spirit continues to lead believers into truth and to progress apprehension of the entailments of truth.

4. Pinnock, *Flame of Love*, 226.
5. Pinnock, *Flame of Love*, 226.
6. Pinnock, *Flame of Love*, 226.
7. Pinnock, *Tracking the Maze*, 171.
8. Pinnock, *Flame of Love*, 226.
9. Pinnock, *Flame of Love*, 226.
10. Pinnock, *Flame of Love*, 223.

Like many well-known theologians before him, Pinnock changed his mind on several issues throughout his career. Though some have tried to discredit his work based on this fact, his willingness to change his mind puts him in the company of leading figures within the Christian theological tradition.[11] And as one might expect, Pinnock's openness to changing his opinion arises from his theological convictions on revelation. Since revelation is not a closed system of propositional truths but "a divine self-disclosure that continues to open up and challenge," humanity can grow and develop in their understanding.[12] Though we grasp it in part, we do not understand its significance entirely. Pinnock states it this way: "the words of Jesus are quantitatively complete, not needing additions, but they are not qualitatively grasped—they need pondering."[13] This means that we obtain greater revelation through the personal leading and guiding of the Spirit. Living in faithfulness to it means faithfulness to God himself.[14]

But we must participate with God in our grasping of truth. Though revelation is by divine initiative, our apprehension *of* it and development *in* it is partially dependent upon us. Growth in revelation is not automatic. God has decided that "divine initiatives and human responses come together in it."[15] God always respects our freedom as to whether we receive and grow in understanding of his revealed character and purposes. As a result, we can either acknowledge or ignore God's prevenient awakening and self-disclosure.[16]

This does not, however, imply that progress is inevitable. Pinnock is clear on the fact that "early thoughts may well be superior to recent ones."[17] Regression, too, is a possibility. Therefore, reliance on God is paramount. As fragile and finite creatures, we are easily deceived and never beyond falling into error. This ought to

11. St. Augustine, for instance. See Gathercole, "Conversion of Augustine."

12. Pinnock, *Flame of Love*, 221.

13. Pinnock, *Flame of Love*, 221.

14. Pinnock, *Flame of Love*, 227.

15. Pinnock, *Tracking the Maze*, 171.

16. Prevenient or enabling grace is divine grace that precedes human decision.

17. Pinnock, *Flame of Love*, 223.

produce both dependence and humility, for both are fundamental for "growing as hearers."[18] If we are indeed following the Spirit, we will sometimes be required to change course since our grasp on revelation is neither "complete nor absolute."[19]

SOURCES OF REVELATION

To disclose the revelation found in Jesus, God has supplied "vehicles of revelation" that facilitate its enactment throughout history.[20] Pinnock believes there are four sources of revelation: Christ is revealed in "a written form (Scripture), a remembering community (tradition), a process of subjective appropriation (experience), and testing for internal consistency (reason)."[21] Therefore, God has chosen to disclose himself within the recording of sacred writings, passed down through the generations, while prompting experiential reception and rational meditations on said sacred writings.[22] Pinnock notes that this understanding of revelation is often known as the "Wesleyan quadrilateral." In such a framework, these revelatory sources conversate amongst one another and illuminate truth. However, Pinnock does not envision the *quadrilateral* to function as an *equilateral.* Rather, Scripture is understood as the primary source above the others. Therefore, in discerning revelation, he privileges Scripture "within a trilateral hermeneutic of tradition, reason, and experience."[23]

Scripture

Roger Olson has noted that Pinnock considers "Scripture as witness to revelation that participates in revelation."[24] Put another way, Pin-

18. Pinnock, *Flame of Love*, 219.
19. Pinnock, *Flame of Love*, 223.
20. Pinnock, *Tracking the Maze*, 171.
21. Pinnock, *Tracking the Maze*, 171.
22. Pinnock, *Tracking the Maze*, 171.
23. Pinnock, "Biblical Texts," 136.
24. Olson, "Postconservative Evangelical Theology," 28.

nock believes Jesus Christ must be the highest form of revelation, and thus refuses to equate the Bible with revelation itself. However, Pinnock still considers Scripture the "norm" of theology considering it supplies believers' access to the original revelation.[25] In Pinnock's words, Scripture "as the Spirit's text enjoys a privileged position. We give it our full consent and pledge ourselves to observe its truth. Every other claim to revelation and development of doctrine is tested by it and must be shown to be included in it."[26] Without the biblical canon, people would reinvent confessions "as they go and adapt it unwisely to the spirit of every age."[27] In this way, Pinnock believes Scripture is significant in that it gives mediated access to the original Christian witness and testimony.

Pinnock's view of revelation also initiated debate over common terminology within Evangelical circles. As such, he was often entangled in discussions over the meaning of terms such as "inerrancy," "inspiration," and "infalliblity." In the end, Pinnock concluded that these terms are not all that helpful. He came to see that "the Bible seldom talks about its 'authority,' and it says nothing at all about its 'inerrancy.'"[28] Because Scripture does not provide a doctrine of its own authority and its "witness on the subject is unsystematic and somewhat fragmentary,"[29] it makes little sense to stretch the scriptural witness in order to make room for these categories.[30]

Yet, despite their limitations, Pinnock still appropriates these terms at times, though he seeks to redefine them in accordance with the way Scripture speaks. He believes that the Bible's own testimony is more modest in its claim to authority, "speaking more about its

25. Pinnock and Brown, *Theological Crossfire*, 40.

26. Pinnock, *Flame of Love*, 229.

27. Pinnock and Brown, *Theological Crossfire*, 40.

28. Pinnock, "New Dimensions,"204.

29. Pinnock, *Scripture Principle*, 54.

30. Pinnock, "New Dimensions," 204. He also notes that his book, *The Scripture Principle*, was his attempt at a "scaled-down theory of inspiration and a more nuanced model of authority" than the earlier one he learned from B. B. Warfield, who, in his mind, "had exaggerated these categories for reasons of the systematic picture he favored (204)."

complete profitability rather than any scholastic perfection."[31] More than anything, it exists to tell the Christian story and to testify to the salvific work of Christ.[32] Pinnock fears that some Evangelicals have tended to treat the Bible as "an end in itself."[33] As a result, the inspiration of Scripture has been inflated "up to a level where it actually rivals Jesus Christ."[34] Properly understood, the Bible does not seek to bear witness to itself, but rather Christ himself.

For Pinnock, the issue is not whether Scripture is authoritative. The issue is what sort of authority it has and what sort of truth it communicates.[35] Rather than merely reflecting on Scripture's *nature*, Pinnock also sees the need to reflect on its *function*. Put another way, rather than only talking about Scripture "from above," Pinnock suggests that we should also talk about Scripture "from below," by concentrating on its usefulness. More than a book of revelatory truth, the Bible is also a "book that feeds and equips the believing community."[36] In addition to a "deposit of truth" it is also a "source of sustenance."[37] The purpose of Scripture is quite pragmatic:

> Claims for the inspiration of Scripture in the Bible are practical and functional more than theoretical. Paul speaks very practically when he says that the Scriptures were given by the Holy Spirit to instruct us for salvation and to equip us for good works (2 Tim 3:15–17). His emphasis is on the profitability, not the inerrancy, of the text, for he sees Scripture more as a means of grace than as an encyclopedia of information.[38]

31. Pinnock and Brown, *Theological Crossfire*, 41.
32. Pinnock, *Tracking the Maze*, 172.
33. Pinnock, *Tracking the Maze*, 175.
34. Pinnock, *Tracking the Maze*, 175.
35. Pinnock and Brow, *Unbounded Love*, 161.
36. Pinnock and Brow, *Unbounded Love*, 162.
37. Pinnock and Brow, *Unbounded Love*, 162.
38. Pinnock and Brow, *Unbounded Love*, 161.

The Bible's overall purpose is to lead people into knowing and loving God.[39] Because of the Spirit's presence in our lives, Christians ought to expect an encounter with the divine in Scripture. Through it, God both instructs and empowers. God has gifted his people with Scripture as a source of authority *and* "as a nourishment" for life with God.[40]

Pinnock contends that by circumventing discussion around the Bible's usefulness, there has been a tendency among Evangelicals "to exaggerate the absolute perfection of the text and minimize the true humanity of it."[41] Divine inspiration has too often been "over-supernaturalized."[42] According to Pinnock, the tendency to interpret the Bible as a nonhuman book is totally misguided. He rightly notes the connection between the doctrines of God, creation, and Scripture. Those who envision God controlling "everything that happens in the world, is very well suited to explain a verbally inspired Bible."[43] However, considering Pinnock's relational theology, which includes—among other things—a conception of divine self-limitation and creaturely autonomy, he opts instead for a dynamic, personal model of Scripture "that upholds both the divine initiative and the human response."[44]

This means that Pinnock seeks to "allow for a human element in the composition of Scripture, but also a strong role for the Spirit to ensure that the truth is not distorted by human receptors."[45] Pinnock does not deny that one will find evidence of humanity in the Bible. Nonetheless, despite the humanness of its witness, the Bible is supremely profitable. Our hope, then, rests on Scripture's claims regarding what God is doing to save humanity and not on every single feature of the witnessing document.[46] Nonetheless, we are

39. Pinnock, *Scripture Principle*, 55.
40. Pinnock and Brow, *Unbounded Love*, 162.
41. Pinnock, *Scripture Principle*, xii.
42. Pinnock, *Tracking the Maze*, 175.
43. Pinnock, *Scripture Principle*, 101.
44. Pinnock, *Scripture Principle*, 103–4.
45. Pinnock, *Scripture Principle*, 103–4.
46. Pinnock, *Tracking the Maze*, 173.

still left with the question, "how do we interpret the Scriptures?"[47] Though the Bible's authority is important, equally important is the conclusion about the kind of text it is and how to use it.[48] Scripture is infallible, but our interpretations are not.[49] Therefore, in order to consistently profit from Scripture, we must become responsible interpreters.

Pinnock offers a two-fold model for interpreting Scripture. "First, we listen to the text as God's Word in human language given to us, and second, we open ourselves to God's Spirit to reveal the particular significance the text has for the present situation."[50] Thus, Pinnock emphasizes both the objective and subjective dimensions of scriptural interpretation. He underscores the importance of attempting to discern what the original authors were intending to communicate. In Pinnock's understanding, Christians need to "uphold the primacy of their intended meaning because we respect these writers as inspired by God and want to know what they had to say."[51] This suggests that "texts of the Bible do have definite meanings in the historical situation and that meaning is the anchor of our interpretation."[52] Further,

> Interpretation is not laying new foundations or establishing new meanings. Any valid interpretation must be congruent with Scripture and must not twist it. . . . Despite the literary theories of postmodernity, a text does not mean anything but something definite. Our goal is to find out what that is and to ask the Spirit to open up the dimensions of its significance. We need it to point out the sins of our culture, to indicate the direction of our mission and to lead us to the implications of doctrine.[53]

47. Pinnock and Brow, *Unbounded Love*, 162.
48. Pinnock, "Biblical Texts," 145.
49. Pinnock and Brow, *Unbounded Love*, 167.
50. Pinnock, *Scripture Principle*, 197.
51. Pinnock and Brow, *Unbounded Love*, 162–63.
52. Pinnock, "Work of the Spirit," 165.
53. Pinnock, *Flame of Love*, 230.

In Pinnock's vision, Scripture must be read within its own context. He does not promote an "uncontrolled subjectivity" in interpretation which might supplant biblical authority.[54] He believes it is essential for readers "to be self-critical and take action against the danger of Scripture-twisting."[55]

Yet, the total meaning of a text cannot be "restricted" to the author's original meaning.[56] On Pinnock's account, "the meaning of texts is not limited to the meaning intended by the authors."[57] Any given text is open to a range of possible meanings because of the Spirit. Pinnock notes that this is demonstrated in Scripture, itself. For instance, New Testament writers often read the Old Testament "in light of the new situation created by the coming of Jesus Christ and the Spirit," which resulted in their interpretations differing from "the grammatical-historical meaning of the text."[58] Often New Testament writers gave texts cited from the Old Testament "a christological twist."[59]

Through the Spirit's leading, one might be able to discern a deeper meaning, intended by God, but not expressed by a human author. The Spirit does not always "play by the exegetical rules."[60] Because of this fact, Pinnock charges Evangelical scholars with being more "interested in inspiration than illumination."[61] By employing this logic, many people fear that emphasizing illumination might lead toward "unbridled subjectivism and reader-driven interpretation."[62] As a result, many Evangelicals would rather emphasize historical exegesis and disregard the reader's role in interpretation altogether. However, Pinnock wishes to show that this is naïve given the fact that all readers, whether they are aware of it

54. Pinnock, "Biblical Texts," 144.
55. Pinnock, "How I Use the Bible," 30.
56. Pinnock, "Work of the Spirit," 165.
57. Pinnock, "Work of the Spirit," 167.
58. Pinnock, "Work of the Holy Spirit," 13.
59. Pinnock, "Work of the Holy Spirit," 13.
60. Pinnock, "Role of the Spirit in Interpretation," 496.
61. Pinnock, "Role of the Spirit in Interpretation," 492.
62. Pinnock, "Role of the Spirit in Interpretation," 492.

or not, are bringing personal interests and presuppositions to the text. Perfect objectivity is not something we can fully achieve, even "though it is an ideal we can strive for by consciously opening ourselves to criticism and correction."[63] Even so, Pinnock thinks that without paying attention to the Spirit, our exegetical work is in vain.[64]

Further, scriptural interpretation is a spiritual exercise, rather than a scientific one: "Having inspired the text and guided the people of God to a canon, the Spirit continues to open up its meaning to us."[65] The Spirit, rather than giving the reader new information, is personally communicating with the reader to provide a fuller conception of the truth that is embedded within the text.[66] Pinnock calls this type of scriptural interpretation "Spirit-hermeneutics":

> Spirit opens up what is written in a controlled liberty of interpretation. To ignore past inspiration would be to risk heresy by straying outside the field of play. To ignore present inspiration would be to risk dead orthodoxy by neglecting what is crucial and timely. God gives us freedom to operate within biblical boundaries by the Spirit, who inspired the witnesses and also opens the significance of scriptural words.[67]

Pinnock, as we have seen, believes that the same Spirit who inspired the scriptural authors breathes new life and significance on their words for the contemporary reader. The Spirit, then, is able to "fuse" the past and present horizons. Pinnock does admit the possibility that Spirit-hermeneutics could be abused, but he considers the possible danger worth it in the end. What is scriptural

63. Pinnock, "How I Use the Bible," 30. Pinnock believes that one reason Evangelicals have failed to adequately enter the science and religion dialogue is due to misreadings of Genesis. As he sees it, Evangelicals must "begin reading early Genesis appropriately in its own context, in the setting of the life of ancient Israel, and to stop forcing modern agendas upon it." See Pinnock, "Climbing Out of a Swamp," 147.

64. Pinnock, "Role of the Spirit in Interpretation," 491.

65. Pinnock, "Biblical Texts," 143.

66. Pinnock, "Biblical Texts," 143.

67. Pinnock, *Flame of Love*, 230.

interpretation without listening to the Spirit? In his understanding, there is an even greater danger in excluding the Spirit from the work of scriptural interpretation. As he puts it, "the relative and oft noted silence about illumination among Evangelicals is suggestive of a certain rationalism. We have to learn to trust the Spirit-empowered Word more and not be so afraid of it."[68] Through the Spirit's illumination, Scripture is alive and active. As we are seized by the Spirit, we can become seized by the text. The Spirit opens our eyes, ears, and hearts to discern Christ's will.[69] Readers, then, should "meditate on Scripture," let it "take root," and let it "become something personal."[70]

But Pinnock begs a pressing question: "Are there any safeguards with Spirit-hermeneutics?"[71] He proposes a few. He insists that the greatest safeguard is the authority discerning community. Because it is easy to hear only what we want to hear, readers of Scripture should listen to others within the Christian community. Often, the Spirit will use others to challenge our own readings of Scripture. This includes allowing "ourselves to be open to the readings of Scripture by other churches in contexts different from our own."[72] Further, Pinnock also notes that God raises up leaders in church communities, to exercise godly leadership which can spare the congregation pain.

Tradition

"Scripture may be *prima* for theology but is not *sola* because tradition plays a role in interpretation."[73] This statement reveals that, in Pinnock's view, Scripture—though primary—is not the only source needed for interpretation and theologizing. The historic Christian tradition must also be consulted. Pinnock defines tradition as "the

68. Pinnock, "Biblical Texts," 144.
69. Pinnock, "Work of the Spirit," 164.
70. Pinnock and Brow, *Unbounded Love*, 164.
71. Pinnock, "Work of the Spirit," 168.
72. Pinnock, "Biblical Texts," 145.
73. Pinnock, *Most Moved Mover*, 21.

process of interpretative transmission."[74] At its best, tradition is not "something archaic and cold" but rather "the living transmission and interpretation of the Scriptures in the churches."[75]

Pinnock notes that, overall, Evangelicals do not highly esteem tradition. Rather, they often prefer to emphasize biblical inspiration while excluding tradition's influence. He wishes to show that this is unwise.[76] The minimization of tradition has made many unaware of its implicit impact on their exegesis. Interpreters are always "deeply affected by tradition, even when we are unaware of it, perhaps especially then."[77] Evangelicals must move away from associating tradition with mere traditionalism. A right view of tradition understands it as an ongoing vehicle of revelation. The Scriptures must then be read in conversation with the Christian theological tradition:

> Let us not read the Bible in isolation but in the context of the historical community. Let us read it with the creeds, liturgical practices and teachings of the fathers in mind. This is being attentive to the presence of the Spirit in the church and having a sense of living community.[78]

Pinnock understands the Spirit leading the Christian community throughout all time into all truth. In fact, the biblical canon itself is a result of the Spirit's leading and working throughout Christian history. Recognizing the importance of tradition is vital to understanding how God is working to reveal Godself throughout the ages. We exist as individuals in a historical community with countless others—both past and present—whose insights guide and inform our own.[79] Scripture should not be read in isolation, for when we consult tradition, we find a "rich comprehension of the original text" which can direct and instruct our own readings.[80]

74. Pinnock, *Tracking the Maze*, 177.
75. Pinnock and Brown, *Theological Crossfire*, 42.
76. Pinnock and Brown, *Theological Crossfire*, 41.
77. Pinnock and Brown, *Theological Crossfire*, 41.
78. Pinnock, *Flame of Love*, 233.
79. Pinnock, *Tracking the Maze*, 177.
80. Pinnock, "How I Use the Bible," 34.

Tradition also helps combat heretical "lost-sight-of exegetical insights."[81] The Creed's of the church universal, "though not infallible," provide guidance in addressing exegetical and theological novelties.[82] Past conclusions alert us to promising directions and potential dangers. Tradition helps the modern reader discern what is legitimate and what is not. However, since Pinnock understands the church as a "pilgrim community traveling toward the future," he believes how we think about doctrines and practices is "always subject to reconsideration" in light of richer understandings of the biblical text.[83] Pinnock is clear: "it ought to be the exception, not the rule, that a conflict would exist between Scripture and tradition."[84] But, when a conflict does occur, Scripture carries primacy over tradition. He explains it this way:

> The biblical faith is never found apart from tradition . . . (but) tradition never mirrors purely and perfectly the truth of the gospel, and it always needs to be monitored by God's word. Tradition is a wonderful servant but a poor master. It serves the church in many ways. But it does not share the same plane with the Scripture. It can and should be placed beneath the Bible and corrected when necessary by the biblical message when it becomes corrupted or complacent.[85]

The text should always be allowed to reform and renew the church and its theology, when necessary. In his view, a genuine development beyond the tradition "would preserve the original idea of a doctrine" but revise it in light of Scripture.[86] With Scripture as a guide, at times, tradition must be "re-oriented to the gospel."[87] Sometimes this will mean taking a fresh interpretive step, one that

81. Pinnock, "How I Use the Bible," 34.
82. Pinnock, "How I Use the Bible," 34.
83. Pinnock, *Flame of Love*, 220.
84. Pinnock, *Flame of Love*, 234.
85. Pinnock, "How I Use the Bible," 34.
86. Pinnock, *Flame of Love*, 235.
87. Pinnock, *Most Moved Mover*, 22.

even challenges the status quo. Though tradition is vital, it must be "continually scrutinized for soundness and relevance."[88]

As mentioned previously, Pinnock's perceived conflict between Scripture and tradition on the doctrine of God led him to reject the moves of "classical theism" for a more dynamic and relational account of God. However, his lifting up of the sacraments is one example in which the weight of tradition influenced a development in his own theology.[89] Frank Macchia has rightly noted that Pinnock believes Evangelicalism's reluctance to embrace tradition has deprived the movement from a "rich variety of insights."[90] Yet, Pinnock also states that there is a "dark side of tradition" which has the "capacity to mislead."[91] Therefore, by promoting tradition while situating it under Scripture, Pinnock believes the church will be able to rediscover old truths without its realities becoming fossilized and unquestionable.

Experience

Overall, Pinnock is quite positive about the role of experience in the Christian life. Christianity is more than a "doctrinal affair."[92] It is "profoundly experiential."[93] Pinnock even exclaims that "the miracle of encountering God cannot be replaced by anything else."[94] It is not enough for the Christian to "believe in the whole counsel of God," but one also must "experience the reality of the gospel."[95] In fact, everyday life should, in some sense, provide "experiential confirmation of the reliability of the truth of the Christian story."[96]

88. Pinnock, *Most Moved Mover*, 22.
89. Pinnock, *Flame of Love*, 240.
90. Macchia, "Tradition and the *Novum*," 33.
91. Macchia, "Tradition and the *Novum*," 33.
92. Pinnock, *Three Keys*, 38.
93. Pinnock, *Three Keys*, 38.
94. Pinnock, *Flame of Love*, 172.
95. Pinnock, *Three Keys*, 37.
96. Pinnock, *Tracking the Maze*, 178.

Given Pinnock's emphasis upon Christian experience, it is fitting that he also understands it to be an important source when doing theology. Both tradition and personal experience are valid "modes of receiving and pondering the Word of God that has come to us through the Scriptures."[97] Tradition, which Pinnock understands as "past experience,"[98] paired with present, personal experience, ought to shape the way we engage Scripture when seeking to construct theology. Yet, "something is seriously wrong when individual experience is pitted against tradition, when experience leads people to reject the witness of Scripture and tradition."[99] By making this claim, Pinnock attempts to show the danger of promoting experience over and above other sources. He seeks to avoid this danger by placing experience in dialogue with tradition and Scripture, while warning of its tendency, at times, to dominate the conversation. One way of curtailing this impulse is to promote Scripture above all other sources. Here Pinnock proposes that Scripture, along with tradition, ought to be forming our experiences.[100] Still, Pinnock acknowledges that it is never that simple. He rightly discerns that experience "played a role in God's giving of revelation in ancient times."[101] In fact, he states that it "was and is always involved."[102]

Steven Studebaker has stated that Pinnock believes, to some degree, that experience ought to shape theological formulations. For example, Pinnock states that Pentecostals should consider that "the Pentecostal way of experiencing God should shape the content of their theology."[103] Pinnock supposes that "Pentecostals are now

97. Pinnock and Brown, *Theological Crossfire*, 43.

98. Pinnock and Brown, *Theological Crossfire*, 42.

99. Pinnock, *Tracking the Maze*, 178.

100. Pinnock and Brown, *Theological Crossfire*, 43,

101. Pinnock and Brown, *Theological Crossfire*, 43,

102. Pinnock and Brown, *Theological Crossfire*, 43,

103. Studebaker, "Clark H. Pinnock," 22. Speaking of the Pentecostal movement, Pinnock states, "The new Pentecostal movement seems to this observer to be a genuine movement of the Spirit of God renewing his church. . . . From these experiences I have emerged a stronger and better Christian." See Pinnock, "New Pentecostalism."

in a strong position to make contributions to theology, distinctive contributions reflecting their own ethos and experience."[104] He exhorts Pentecostals for drawing a connection between theology and spirituality,[105] and urges them to abstain from Evangelical rationalistic approaches.[106] Instead, he invites them to continue to mine the interrelationship between experience and theology:

> Conservative-Evangelicals lean in the direction of scholasticism, viewing theology as a rational discipline, somewhat apart from the life of piety. Pietists on the other hand see the message as more a centrally life changing narrative than a matter of assenting to doctrines. . . . While scholasticism tends to protect the "objective" truth of Scripture from contamination by "subjective" experience, pietists insist that experience is of itself very important. I am learning not to place doctrine over experience or experience over doctrine but to reject the objective/subjective dualism and seek to integrate the two.[107]

Revelation has experiential and cognitive aspects to it: "we must know God experientially, not just cognitively."[108] The task of theology requires both mind and heart—study and prayer.[109] The aim is to forge a balanced approach by insisting upon a model of revelation "which includes propositional communication as well as personal communion."[110] As we should expect from Pinnock, he exhorts readers to move beyond "extreme" positions:

> One the one hand, liberal theology views revelation in relation to human experience rather than as historical and cognitive. In this view revelation is not tied down to its content but is viewed as a transforming event that sets

104. Pinnock, "Divine Relationality,"4.

105. Pinnock, "Divine Relationality," 11. In particular, Pinnock urges Pentecostals to make explicit what is implicit within their spirituality: a relational model of God (23).

106. Pinnock, *Three Keys*, 37.

107. Pinnock, "Confessions," 388.

108. Pinnock, *Flame of Love*, 170.

109. Pinnock, *Flame of Love*, 12.

110. Pinnock, *Scripture Principle*, 27.

> people free . . . on the other hand, evangelical theology errs on the other side. It very often views revelation in terms of timeless, propositional content.[111]

Pinnock wants to give weight to both the objective and the subjective modes of truth, for in his mind, "revelation is dynamic, historical and personal."[112]

As I noted earlier, when doing theology Pinnock privileges Scripture within a trilateral hermeneutic of tradition, experience, and reason. This means that, in some cases, personal experience can subvert past experience—tradition—if it makes better sense of Scripture. Put another way, traditional formulations can and should be modified if such a revisioning will prove to be more "credible in practical terms" while also remaining "biblically and rationally sound."[113] Therefore, doctrines should be concerned about "the existential fit" and practical viability to meet the needs of life.[114]

Reason

Even God's own self-disclosure must be "thought out and not left undigested."[115] Truth must be articulated coherently and intelligibly. Theological concepts are expected to be "internally consistent and coherent" with other beliefs held.[116] Though reason is a human faculty, and its role is modest, God has created humanity with the desire for intelligibility. Thus, reason in theology can function to assist with critical analysis and formulating God's truth with systematic integrity.[117] Therefore, Pinnock values the contribution that philosophy and reason can make to theology.[118]

111. Pinnock, *Flame of Love*, 224–25.
112. Pinnock, *Flame of Love*, 227.
113. Pinnock, *Most Moved Mover*, 153.
114. Pinnock, *Most Moved Mover*, 23.
115. Pinnock and Brown, *Theological Crossfire*, 42.
116. Pinnock, *Most Moved Mover*, 22.
117. Pinnock, *Tracking the Maze*, 179.
118. Pinnock, *Most Moved Mover*, 22.

Pinnock proposes that philosophy can often help provide categories to help theologians express what needs to be said "on the basis of revelation."[119] However, Pinnock is convinced that philosophy can often be given too much of a role in theology. For example, he holds that much of traditional Catholic theology has been excessively influenced by Thomistic thinking, while much of modern Protestant thinking has been overly conditioned by process thought. In some cases, an overdependence upon philosophy and reason can hinder one's handling of revelation. What is needed, then, is prudent caution and discernment when determining "which philosophical resources serve the proclamation and which hinder it."[120] His overall advice for theologians is to "enter with care into dialogue with philosophy, ancient and modern, and make the best use of it we can."[121]

Nonetheless, Pinnock is generally positive about the role philosophy can play in expressing revelatory truths. But he is quick to state that not all philosophical systems are equally accommodating. For instance, he is overall critical of Platonic and Aristotelian philosophical categories in theology, though he does find strengths in Greek thinking that have greatly assisted historic Christian theology. He states that despite the drawbacks, "it was a responsible decision" for early theologians to utilize Hellenistic thinking.[122] He recognizes that all people are historically influenced. Therefore, Pinnock argues that "we all do metaphysics" and "we are all influenced by philosophy"[123]

Considering Pinnock's hope for the scriptural message to be relevant to contemporary people, he prefers to utilize "categories familiar to this new world."[124] Therefore, he prefers dynamic and relational categories for theology since he believes they better express the personal reality of God. He aims, then, to situate revelation

119. Pinnock, *Most Moved Mover*, 22.

120. Pinnock, *Most Moved Mover*, 23.

121. Pinnock, *Most Moved Mover*, 23.

122. Pinnock, *Most Moved Mover*, 116.

123. Pinnock, *Most Moved Mover*, 116, 150.

124. Pinnock, *Tracking the Maze*, 179.

within a framework that is both scripturally sound and conceptually adequate for contemporary times.

Finally, Pinnock is positive about reason's role in theology, but he also acknowledges the limitations of human language and intellect:

> It is not Christian to view reason as an autonomous, omnicompetent, or final judge of truth, as if it were neutral or independent of other social, historical, and relational modes of knowing. Faith seeks to understand its own intrinsic intelligibility, but it also respects mystery and is aware of the limits of reason's ability to understand divine truth.[125]

Reason is a resource for formulating and communicating God's self-disclosure. As we will soon discuss in the following chapter, Pinnock advocates for the role of science in discerning truth. Still, Pinnock believes there are limitations when employing finite resources to realize the infinite.[126] Though we should not shy away from speaking positively about God given his self-disclosure, we ought to do so with great humility and care.

CONCLUSION

In sum, Pinnock believes that Jesus Christ is the supreme and ultimate revelation (Heb 1:3), and that God has chosen to disclose the revelation of Jesus Christ within the recording of Scripture, passed down through the generations, while prompting experiential reception and rational meditations. Therefore, Pinnock finds the Wesleyan quadrilateral as a helpful model for organizing these "sources" of revelation. However, this way of understanding revelation is different from some of Pinnock's earliest formulations. Between his works *A Defense of Biblical Infallibility* (1967) and *The*

125. Pinnock, *Tracking the Maze*, 179.

126. As mentioned previously, Pinnock described himself shifting "from hard to soft rationality" over his career. He says the result is that he became "less hardline" and "more open to dialogue" as time went on. See Pinnock, "Pinnock Postscript," 229.

Scripture Principle (1984), Pinnock moved from a "philosophical biblicism" to a "simple biblicism." As he perceives it, Pinnock considered his move to be from a fundamentalist form of strict inerrancy, to a more nuanced, although still revelationally established view of Scripture. In other words, Pinnock considered his change to be one marked by a journey from the margin to the center.

Later reflecting on this change, Pinnock stated that though some were appreciative of a more realistic doctrine of biblical inspiration, many were not.[127] Callen rightly notes that Pinnock quickly realized he was "walking a tightrope, explaining to the liberals why so few revisions were being made and to the fundamentalists why there were so many."[128] For instance, Pinnock's *The Scripture Principle* was reviewed critically by both liberal theologians and conservative theologians. James Barr claimed that Pinnock did not go far enough in his revisions, while Roger Nicole accused Pinnock of going too far.[129] Wesleyan theologian Randy Maddox's comments on the work sees it as an attempt to construct a mediating position between these poles.[130] Though Maddox finds points of disagreement, he believes Pinnock succeeds in providing a highly nuanced and critically aware articulation of scriptural authority.

Thus, it seems that—once again—Pinnock finds himself between two "extremes," holding to middle ground when it comes to the issue of God's revelation.

127. Pinnock, "Pinnock Postscript," 237.

128. Callen, *Journey Toward Renewal*, 57.

129. See Barr, "Review," 37; Nicole, "Clark Pinnock's Precarious Balance," 68.

130. Maddox, "Review," 204–7.

3

Creation: Open & Free

WHY IS THERE A creation at all? Certainly, God has no need—God is wholly fulfilled within his own trinitarian life. Still, creation exists. What might we make of this? In Pinnock's view, creation does not exist due to a lack on God's part, but rather because of God's generosity: "God is pure ecstasy—each Person exists in loving relationship with the other Persons, and the joyous fellowship spills over into giving life to the creature."[1] As a relational being, the triune God creates and brings forth life out of his own bountiful, interpersonal love. Since God is love, he desires to bring forth a world with creatures that are capable of loving God and other creatures.[2] In this way, God does not hoard his relational life, but seeks to share it with his creation so that he may delight in it. God creates for his own joy, but his joy as lover is to admit new partners into God's own life. However, because God creates out love, he gifts all his creation—both animate and inanimate—with freedom. And in working with *and* within creation, the Spirit draws it toward its goal of resurrection.

1. Pinnock, *Flame of Love*, 55.
2. Pinnock, "Great Jubilee," 94.

THE CREATOR/CREATION RELATIONSHIP

Creation is a piece of divine self-expression. Though "ontologically distinct, God enters into the world and receives pleasure and derives value from it."[3] To be clear: Pinnock envisions God receiving pleasure *from* creation *for* creation's sake, since he has no lack within his trinitarian life. Further, God has created everything distinct from himself, but has invited it to participate within his own relational life. Pinnock puts it this way: "Creation exists on another level of being from God but is not in every sense outside of God."[4] Essential to this understanding is Pinnock's pneumatology. As the Nicene Creed states, the Spirit is the "Lord and giver of life," which applies to all of life.[5] Following Irenaeus, Pinnock understands the Spirit—along with the Word—to be the two hands of God. Together they operate and cooperate in a mutual manner. Therefore, "the Word is the source of the cosmic order and the Spirit is the supervisory engineer monitoring the development of the creation with an eye to the future."[6] Pinnock states that it was St. Basil who rightly conceived the Spirit as involved with the creation of "the nonhuman universe and as fostering and enabling emergence of the world and as giving it its grace and beauty."[7] Therefore, the Spirit—as the power of creation—is both its initiator and sustainer.

Thus, there is no "sacred-secular split,"[8] for the Spirit is present within the whole created order and can make his presence known in and through all things. For too long in Christian history the Spirit has been understood to be related only to church and piety.[9] An important concept within Scripture is that the Spirit is the universal divine presence. As such, God initiated creation through the Spirit and continues to work with creation as its director. As it moves toward its goal, the Spirit groans with creation as it longs for

3. Pinnock, *Flame of Love*, 57.
4. Pinnock, *Flame of Love*, 58.
5. Pinnock, "Other Hand of God," 207.
6. Pinnock, "Other Hand of God," 206.
7. Pinnock, "Other Hand of God," 209.
8. Pinnock, *Flame of Love*, 62.
9. Pinnock, *Flame of Love*, 49.

deliverance from its current bondage. And because the Spirit is at the center of all God's working within the created order, we can encounter God's presence "in, with, and beneath life's experiences."[10] Thus, God is indeed related to his world through the Spirit. However, how might we best understand this relationship?

Pinnock as a rule contends that God is neither distant *from* the world, nor exercising tyrannical, all-determining power *over* the world. While God is not the world and the world is not God, "God is in the world and the world is in him."[11] God is other than the world, but by God's choosing, the world shares in the life of God. In seeking to posit a tension between God's transcendence and immanence, Pinnock intimately relates God to the world, without conjoining them:

> Because God transcends space and time, while being fully present to it, we may think of the universe developing within the life of God. This happens in such a way that it impacts God as well as having God impact it. The fundamental character of reality is relational in God and creation; the world can be seen as developing within God and within the trinitarian relations of mutual love. Though he is "Lord," the Spirit is also immanent in the world and can deal with it, not just from the "outside" but from the "inside" too. In effect the world develops within dynamic relations of the divine communion.[12]

Pinnock suggests that God has chosen to work within his creation, while also being distinct from it. In this way, he aims to develop a dynamic, relational model of the exchange between Creator and creation. While some have accused him of blurring the lines between God and the world, one might consider that Pinnock is seeking to find a middle position between classical theism's one-sidedness in the direction of transcendence, and process theism's equally one-sidedness toward radical immanence. He surely agrees with the fourth century theologian Hilary of Poitiers when he states

10. Pinnock, *Flame of Love*, 61.

11. Pinnock, *Flame of Love*, 61.

12. Pinnock, "Other Hand of God," 212.

that God "is present in all things; in him who is infinite all are included,"[13] and with John of Damascus' (676–749 AD) statement that God "fills all things with his essence . . . but in his power the world does not contain him."[14] Pinnock suggests a model that may keep a "proper balance between transcendence and immanence" as seen in the dynamic biblical presentation and in particular thinkers of the dogmatic tradition.[15]

Indispensable to this understanding of God's relationship to the world is Pinnock's conviction that the act of creation itself was and is an act of divine *kenosis*. In Pinnock's view, we cannot just associate God's self-limitation with the incarnation, but also with creation.[16] God has created the universe out of love, thus limiting the exercise of his own sovereignty in order to relate to the world in love.[17] Pinnock envisions God embracing self-limitations in order that his creation is "not crushed by the divine reality or totally absorbed by it."[18] Within this conception, God interacts with creation but does not overrule its divinely granted freedom to be itself. Though God is the source of all creaturely possibilities, he allows his creation to have liberty and freedom to take its own path, which may in fact work out in a manner that goes against his divine intentions. Out of love, the all-mighty God limits/constrains his use of power so that the world can become a reality other than Godself.[19] Thus, God has chosen to create the world with its own freedom to adapt, evolve, and unfold gradually, according to its own pace.

13. Hilary of Poitiers, "On the Trinity," 1.6.

14. John of Damascus, "Orthodox Faith," 1.13.

15. Pinnock, "Between Classical and Process Theism," 313–14.

16. Pinnock, *Flame of Love*, 61.

17. Pinnock, "Between Classical and Process Theism," 323.

18. Moltmann, "God's *Kenosis*," 145.

19. Pinnock, "Evangelical Theology after Darwin," 105.

THEOLOGY AND SCIENCE

For Pinnock, science and theology are the "two forms of human responses to reality."[20] God's word and his creation are both roads to God's revelation. Rather than viewing them as antithetical, science and theology can complement one another. Hence, "science has important things to say to theology, and theology to science."[21] The book of Scripture and the book of nature ought to cooperate with one another, leading us to a fuller picture of reality. Because theology and science broach God's creation from different vantage points, there is rich opportunity for dialogue between them. The physicist-theologian John Polkinghorne puts it in a way that, I think, Pinnock would agree with: "One must look beyond the insights achieved by the individual disciplines of enquiry, such as science and theology, to seek an integrated account of the whole of reality."[22] Because theologians and scientists both exegete God's world, they should be in dialogue with one another, looking for a mutual enrichment. Theologians can learn from scientists how God is active in natural processes while scientists can learn from theologians how to account for what seems to be a certain kind of intelligence within the created order.

From a theological standpoint, Pinnock believes one way forward in this interaction is to affirm the Spirit's role in creation, which can help provide new opportunities for future dialogues. Suggesting that God is at work in nature bringing about the future of the world in conjunction with natural processes can advance this dialogue between theology and science. As recent science has challenged former assumptions about nature as a determinate and static mechanism, this makes "it possible to make the divine-world relationship more intelligible."[23] As we should expect from Pinnock, this makes possible a belief in the "Creator Spirit" who continues to create, operating within nature and moving it toward its destiny.[24]

20. Pinnock, *Flame of Love*, 64.
21. Pinnock, *Flame of Love*, 64.
22. Polkinghorne, *Science and Religion*, 20.
23. Pinnock, *Flame of Love*, 66.
24. Pinnock, *Flame of Love*, 67.

Because it is difficult to account for the existence of the world within a naturalistic framework, Pinnock considers that belief in the Spirit as the "temporal first cause of the world" helps alleviate this difficulty.[25] This paired with the intelligence of the world—especially nature's capacity to produce relational beings—points to divine agency and a power of ingenuity at work in the universe.[26] Yet, Pinnock is not primarily motivated by scientific theory, but by Scripture instead—which in his reading—broadly asserts that God grants freedom to his whole creation.

CREATION AND DEVELOPMENT

Creation ought not to be identified only in terms of a singular event at the beginning of time. People too often think that God has created the world and has since left it to run on its own. Rather, we ought to understand that the Holy Spirit continues to refine, hone, and sustain the creation:

> We do not need to conceptualize the creation event as a one-time action that produces a world and then ceases to operate. One may image a continual energizing of world by the Spirit throughout its long history (*creatio continua*). I find it helpful to be able to think of the Spirit pervading the universe, knitting things together and holding the world open for divine love.[27]

The way Pinnock frames God's ongoing creative activity helps account for the unanticipated ingenuity that seems to be at work in nature.[28] Understood within this light, the Spirit continues to work within the natural processes through refining and enhancing. This suggest that God's Spirit is the "perfecting source of dynamism evident in the cosmos."[29] The universe is a work in progress rather than

25. Pinnock, *Flame of Love*, 67.
26. Pinnock, *Flame of Love*, 67.
27. Pinnock, "Great Jubilee," 95.
28. Pinnock, *Flame of Love*, 68.
29. Pinnock, *Flame of Love*, 68.

a finished project, for creation is still taking place and the process requires much time in order to realize its promise.[30]

Further, without affirming the Spirit's working within nature, conscious life is especially difficult to account for. Again, Pinnock is worth quoting in full:

> It has become even more difficult to accept on purely naturalistic grounds such realities as human freedom, openness, creativity, rationality and sensitivity to aesthetic, moral and religious values. Something in nature is moving things from simple to complex, from nonliving to living, from unconscious to conscious life, from animal to human.[31]

Therefore, we must understand that the Spirit animates the world, drawing it forward in conjunction with a free creation. This implies that divine action within natural processes is not much as interventions from "the outside," as it is workings from "the inside."[32]

In seeking to side-step what he sees to be the fruitless debates between evolutionism and creationism, Pinnock argues that creationists too often twist science to cohere with their particular conceptions of faith, while certain proponents of macroevolution have twisted science to serve their naturalistic understandings. Both literalistic interpretations of the Bible and strictly naturalistic worldviews contort science toward their predetermined biases. As a result, evolutionists are often blind to design-like features in nature even when it is evident, while on the other hand, creationists disregard the age of the earth and deny the developments in nature since the initial creation.[33] For Pinnock, both of these misrepresentations have failed to recognize the cosmic role of the Spirit's activity.

The better way forward, as Pinnock envisions it, is to develop a theology of creation within the context of pneumatology that takes in account recent scientific findings, especially the contention that nature is free and open to possibilities. Thus, accepting

30. Pinnock, "Evangelical Theology after Darwin," 105.

31. Pinnock, *Flame of Love*, 70.

32. Pinnock, "Other Hand of God," 209.

33. Pinnock, *Flame of Love*, 65.

macroevolution "does not require abandoning belief in God."[34] Overall, Pinnock sees macroevolution as a thoughtful proposal that accounts for substantial bodies of evidence.[35] Rather than a threat to faith, evolution posits opportunities as a putative model that may make sense of how the Creator has gone about his work in the natural world.

As a result, Pinnock urges Evangelicals to follow the lead of "our Catholic brothers and sisters when it comes to considering evolution."[36] In his view, Catholic theologians have worked through the issues of science and theology in careful and constructive ways. Unfortunately, the resentment toward macroevolution among Evangelicals results from embracing poor readings of Scripture and a form of anti-intellectualism. Often, too much time and energy has been given to defending biblical inerrancy than has been given interpreting the Bible "impressively."[37] In his view, Evangelicals have typically failed to read early Genesis appropriately within its own context and setting, and as a result, have forced modern agendas onto the text. Instead, one ought to look for how the creation texts are attempting to speak theologically about "our relationship with God the creator in contrast to systems of dualism and pantheism; the meaning and destiny of our own existence grounded in the purpose of God; the goodness of created lives," and creation as the foundation of the belief in the "intelligibility of the world."[38] Pinnock is clearly not suggesting one ought to transform biblical claims into existential symbols out of convenience, but rather one ought to allow "the Bible to say what it wants to say" without imposing modern programs on it.[39]

Therefore, as the biblical creation texts are read rightly, the broad theory of evolution can become an important conversation partner. Though the theory of evolution "has much to say about

34. Pinnock, "Evangelical Theology after Darwin," 103.
35. Pinnock, "Evangelical Theology after Darwin," 104.
36. Pinnock, "Evangelical Theology after Darwin," 104.
37. Pinnock, "Climbing Out of a Swamp," 144.
38. Pinnock, "Climbing Out of a Swamp," 153.
39. Pinnock, "Climbing Out of a Swamp," 155.

how natural selection preserves and refines organisms once they have appeared, it sheds less light on how and why positive new features originate."[40] This makes way for theologians to help scientists by reflecting on the Spirit's cosmic role within natural processes. Science and theology in dialogue helps us understand that God not only created the world at the beginning but has also endowed his creation with the freedom to develop and adapt over time with the Spirit as its guide. The Spirit continues to create in nature, bringing the world toward its goal. Pinnock believes that gleaning insights from macroevolutionary theory does not imply deism, but instead, suggests that God has "richly endowed the earth with the capacity to move toward the complexities that we see in nature."[41] As the Spirit works within the world, the Spirit creates and seeds the world with new possibilities. This points to the fact that "the fundamental character of reality seems to be relational with entities being interrelated at all levels."[42] Again, in Pinnock's formulation, God has imbued his creation with relationality.

Yet, God is not just present with creation in the past and in the present, but as Pinnock understands it, the Spirit is moving creation toward its future.[43] In fact, the Spirit is preparing us and moving us toward "the great leap to consummation, when life really begins."[44] Creation along with humanity will be set free from all bondage and decay. God will bring sabbath rest to all of creation. Humanity will reach full union with God, and creation will be renewed and restored, though none of this is possible without God's Spirit moving his creation toward this destiny.

40. Pinnock, *Flame of Love*, 68.

41. Pinnock, "Evangelical Theology after Darwin," 103.

42. Pinnock, "Evangelical Theology after Darwin," 105.

43. Here we see a notable difference between Pinnock's open view of the future and process theology. In Pinnock's view, the future has no ontology. The future is always becoming and therefore has no being in and of itself. Thus, Pinnock can speak of God "moving" creation toward the future. On the other hand, process theology posits God as relating to creation from the future, and thus "luring" creation toward its goal, as if from the end working toward the present.

44. Pinnock, *Flame of Love*, 181.

In sum, as God's people pay attention to his activity in the universe, Christians can better appreciate the divine care for the human and nonhuman world. It also provides "a kind of reenchanting of nature."[45] These insights naturally lead to a "spirituality of the present and the ordinary, a celebration of God here with us and our dwelling in God," while also developing a "heart of thanksgiving for creation and every part of it."[46] Understanding God involved in the past, present, and future of creation further helps motivate our care for God's world. Therefore, not only do these conceptions enrich our beliefs, but in Pinnock's understanding, it also enriches our spiritualities and practices.

HUMANITY

God created humanity in his image. Though God loves his whole creation, Pinnock believes that "humanity is the goal of creation," for it is the "glory and goal of the process."[47] All creation is to be respected and revered, but none more than human beings. Humankind has been fashioned with the capacity of having a relationship with the Creator in such a way that it mirrors God's own love to the rest of the created order. Out of all created species, we have been especially endowed with freedom, accountability, and the capability to live altruistically. Clearly God has chosen humanity for rich relationship with him. The Spirit has brought forth the human spirit to enable us to participate in this relationship. All humans are graced with the ability to respond and know God in a distinctive way. The issue is whether humanity welcomes or refuses the Spirit's coming to them.

God formed the world with the capability to bring about human life. Pinnock believes that within the process of creation, the Spirit is working to bring about the emergence of the human "soul." Thus, "the emergence of human soul is not an exception to

45. Pinnock, "Other Hand of God," 209.

46. Pinnock, *Flame of Love*, 66.

47. Pinnock, *Flame of Love*, 71.

the animating process but an intense example of it."[48] The Spirit has worked with and within creation to bring about this outcome. Pinnock believes that the likelihood that conscious, rational, moral, and spiritual beings could have come to exist solely within a natural or random process is unintelligible.[49] In fact, God has gifted humankind with the unique ability to deliberate on the process that God used to bring humanity about: "Though children of the system, we are semi-transcendent to it and able to reflect on it." This exceptional capability affirms the biblical truth that we have been created in the Creator's own likeness. However, Pinnock realizes that there is a cost to the way that God has chosen to bring about creation and humanity into being. Even though the created order is a manifestation of the love of God, it "entails suffering too."[50] As a result, life develops amid pain and death. This implies that nature is not yet finished and is continually in-process.

This all indicates that God is unhurried. The divine plan for forming humans sees death operative before human sin. This forces Pinnock to rethink humanity's "fall." On Pinnock's account, one must understand "death in a different sense: death as the termination of life, which is part of the created order, and death as the ending of human life in fear and guilt, which is not."[51] Within this conceptual framework, the first humans would still have reached the end of life and freely entered into God's presence, yet they would not have died a sinners' death—one that is marked by a distressed conscience.

Because of humanity's fall, the whole creation has been yearning for reconciliation. Pinnock points out that present environmental suffering is either aided or eased by humanity. For too long humanity has wreaked havoc on the world of nature. He urges humanity to consider the value of creation care since the Spirit is the "ecologist par excellence, forming and sustaining all habitable

48. Pinnock, "Evangelical Theology after Darwin," 108.

49. Pinnock, *Flame of Love*, 71.

50. Pinnock, *Flame of Love*, 72.

51. Pinnock, *Flame of Love*, 72.

space."[52] Creation is destined to share in the glory of God, making it blasphemous to do violence to the environment. Nature has been gifted to humanity as its dwelling place and is destined to participate in our reconciliation. Therefore,

> The destruction of nature is hurtful to the God who formed it and loves it. The Spirit suffers along with nature and struggles against powers that despoil. God delights in creation and grieves over its despoliation.[53]

Humanity, then, needs to care for the natural order, rather than exploiting it. In Pinnock's words, "the Spirit calls us to ecological consciousness."[54] By caring for God's creation, we are anticipating God's reconciling of all things.

PROVIDENCE AND THEODICY

Pinnock's doctrine of creation in dialogue with his open view of God provides creative insights for providence and theodicy. God has created an open and dynamic world. As such, God has goals for the world, but not "blueprints."[55] God has a vision for the future but has not fixed it. Perhaps, then—in Pinnock's view—it is best to say that God has chosen to be in charge, without being in control.

Thus, to speak of God's providence does not imply predetermination, but rather God's purposes being worked out in the world alongside cosmic and creaturely freedom. This "kenotic model" of providence insists that God does not coerce his creation, but instead respects its freedom.[56] Though God could have created a world in which he exercised complete control, he instead decided to limit his power for the sake of love. God took risks in creating the world we inhabit; thus, providence often has a "scandalous appearance."[57]

52. Pinnock, *Flame of Love*, 70.
53. Pinnock, *Flame of Love*, 77.
54. Pinnock, *Flame of Love*, 77.
55. Pinnock, "Evangelical Theology after Darwin," 106.
56. Pinnock, "Evangelical Theology after Darwin," 107.
57. Pinnock, *Flame of Love*, 76.

The fact that we live in an unfinished universe should be viewed positively, because without unique, novel events, the cosmos could become "locked into a fixed order,"[58] implying lifelessness and mindlessness. God has chosen, instead, to create a dynamic world rather than a static one. Yes, God is intimately engaged in creation's development, but he is involved without controlling and predetermining its development. Therefore, "we must not be too simplistic in trying to understand how divine care will manifest itself," for "we cannot say exactly how God works in the world."[59] In general terms Pinnock believes it is best to state that the Spirit is the breath of life, animating everything in creation and alluring it toward greater and greater complexity.

But God does not always get his way with creation. Creation acts in ways that are not in keeping with his overall purposes. There are genuine tragedies that takes place within the world that grieve the heart of God and are not a part of some greater good.[60] Because God has endowed the universe with genuine freedom sometimes it will act in ways that are destructive. The paradox of the present order of nature is that of amazing creativity alongside immense suffering. One way Pinnock seeks to deal with this difficulty is to account for a "demonic dimension in evolutionary suffering."[61] Pinnock views evil and destruction as presently at work within humanity and the cosmos. As he envisions it, there is genuine warfare taking place between Christ's kingdom and the kingdom of darkness. Here Pinnock proposes that without taking demonic agency seriously, one is missing an important account of suffering in the world.

Pinnock, too, admits that there is something mysterious about why suffering has played such a prominent role in history. We can take hope, though, that "God shares in the suffering of the evolving creation."[62] God is not apathetic to the pains of the world but has chosen to share in the "birth pangs of nature that anticipate

58. Pinnock, "Evangelical Theology after Darwin," 106.

59. Pinnock, "Evangelical Theology after Darwin,"106.

60. Pinnock, *Most Moved Mover*, 176.

61. Pinnock, "Evangelical Theology after Darwin," 107.

62. Pinnock, "Evangelical Theology after Darwin," 108.

new creation."[63] Only the new creation can put a halt to the current violence, misery, and death. Our hope lies in the fact that God will bring about rest for the entire cosmos. In working with creation, "God is calling the universe to reach beyond itself to new creation."[64] We then trust that the cosmic journey is heading toward a resurrected future.

CONCLUSION

Clark Pinnock's doctrine of creation, as we have seen, is tightly connected to his doctrine of God. Therefore, Pinnock develops a dynamic, relational model of the exchange between Creator and creation. He relates God to the world, without seeking to conjoin them. However, British Evangelical Daniel Strange has stated that though Pinnock does not discard the notion of divine transcendence, Pinnock's claim that God is in the world, and the world is in God,[65] suggests that Pinnock disrupts the "very careful balance between God's transcendence and immanence (in favor of immanence)."[66] Related is the American Evangelical theologian Donald Bloesch's critique that though Pinnock plots a "middle way between process theism and classical theism," he is closer "in some respects to the first."[67] One gets the impression that these fellow Evangelicals believe Pinnock does not place enough emphasis upon the absoluteness of God and overemphasizes God's relatedness to the world.

Process theologians, however, are also quite critical of Pinnock's project, but in the opposite direction. David Ray Griffin, for example, critique's Pinnock's assertion that God has voluntary self-limited his power in relation to his creation.[68] This, in Griffin's mind,

63. Pinnock, "Evangelical Theology after Darwin," 108.

64. Pinnock, "Evangelical Theology after Darwin," 108.

65. Pinnock, *Flame of Love*, 62.

66. Strange, "Presence, Prevenience, or Providence?," 245.

67. Bloesch, *God the Almighty*, 255.

68. Process theologian John Cobb also criticizes Pinnock's idea of God as self-limiting and states that it is better to understand God as metaphysically

implies that God can, at any time, "throw off this self-limitation and take unilateral charge of the outcome of the world."[69] Process theologians, then, are dissatisfied with Pinnock's theodicy since it leaves open the possibility that God has the power to prevent evil, since his limitations are only voluntary and not metaphysically necessary. And though there are more critical assessments that could be noted, I believe these few are enough to demonstrate how Pinnock often frustrates his fellow dialogue partners. This is for sure: his theology does not fit neatly within a longstanding and established tradition. In his own words, Pinnock is a "theological maverick" who wants to imagine "a future where Evangelicals and liberals mature and come around to more sensible middle positions."[70]

---

limited. See Cobb, "Clark Pinnock and Process Theology," 263–65.

69. Griffin, "Process Theology," 33.

70. Pinnock, "Foreword," xvi.

4

Salvation: Union & Universality

Pinnock, as we have seen, repeatedly emphasizes God's relational nature. It is no surprise, then, that Pinnock views salvation in "relational, affective terms."[1] Rather than highlighting justification, he highlights union. Instead of emphasizing forensic acquittal, he emphasizes restored relationship. While salvation is a multifaceted process that includes many dimensions, the "goal is glorification and union with God."[2] This possibility exists for *everyone* because of God's generous love. Salvation is a universal possibility due to the Spirit's activity throughout space and time. However, God is not only interested in saving individuals. Pinnock believes salvation is a broad category encompassing concerns of "both body and soul, individual and society, the material and the spiritual."[3] In other words, God's aim is to save and redeem *all* things through Christ: individuals, communities, and cosmos.[4]

1. Pinnock, *Flame of Love*, 149.
2. Pinnock, *Flame of Love*, 150.
3. Pinnock and Brow, *Unbounded Love*, 112.
4. Pinnock, "Great Jubilee," 99.

A RELATIONAL PROCESS

Pinnock argues for a "non-coercive model of salvation, holding that God relates to us as I-thou not as I-it and that human persons can say 'yes' or 'no' to him."[5] God has taken the initiative by saying "yes" to us in Jesus Christ, yet he also desires "to hear our 'yes' in return (1 John 4:19; 2 Cor 1:19)."[6] Salvation is a gift—to be sure—but it is a gift that can be rejected. While the Christian life from beginning to end is a work of grace, at any point, God's will can be thwarted by believers. Whether one will persevere in God's grace is not a given.[7] This suggests, then, that for Pinnock, "the continuation of salvation depends, in part, on the human partner because the relationship is personal and reciprocal. One perseveres . . . through the power of God."[8] Salvation, then, is essentially cooperative.

The Holy Spirit may draw, but people must also consent. We work out our salvation, while God is at work in us (Phil 2:12–13). Or, to say the same thing a different way, "in conversion there is an interplay of grace and assent."[9] Pinnock envisions God *not* to be all-determining, and his grace not irresistible.[10] Rather, Pinnock takes his lead from the Christian East: "Eastern Orthodoxy has always rejected any doctrine of grace that denies freedom, because freedom is essential to the image of God in us. We require grace to enter fellowship with God, but we have a part to play. Salvation requires the operation of both grace and the human will."[11] He argues that the Greek Fathers before Augustine took this view. Within this framework faith is understood as both "a gift and human act."[12] Though some have attempted to charge him with some form of semi-Pelagianism, Pinnock is clear that:

5. Pinnock, *Most Moved Mover*, 163.
6. Pinnock, *Most Moved Mover*, 163.
7. Pinnock, *Most Moved Mover*, 167.
8. Pinnock, *Most Moved Mover*, 170.
9. Pinnock, *Flame of Love*, 158.
10. Pinnock, *Flame of Love*, 158.
11. Pinnock, *Flame of Love*, 160.
12. Pinnock, *Flame of Love*, 161.

> It is God who saves us; we do not save ourselves. The grace of God at work in us is always preparing us to receive more grace. There is a role for human participation in salvation, but it is grounded in God's gracious empowering not in our inherent abilities. Our cooperation is possible because of God's empowering Spirit working within us.[13]

In Pinnock's understanding, too much emphasis within Western Christian thought has been placed on the sinner's change from guilty to not guilty. Hence, salvation is often only understood within legal terms at the expense of a more personal one. Pinnock envisions a "more relational model" in which the Spirit of God leads humanity to union—"transforming, personal, intimate relationship with the triune God."[14] Salvation is essentially journeying toward and with God. And rather than an event, salvation is an unfolding process, directed by the Spirit of God in which we are invited to participate.

The process of salvation "has a beginning, a middle, and an end."[15] By making such claims, Pinnock challenges all forms of "decisionism" within Evangelicalism that associate salvation or "conversion" with a one-time event. As Pinnock sees it, conversion is a multifaceted process that is associated with faith and baptism.[16] Pentecostal theologian Simon Chan has noted that Pinnock is unique among Protestants in following a sacramental interpretation of Spirit baptism.[17] Though the Spirit is working preveniently prior to one's baptism, the water rite is the place where one receives the Spirit. However, it is not so much that the Spirit is rigidly tied to baptism, but that "baptism is part of a conversion complex in which the Spirit is received."[18] Baptism in the Spirit, which is sacramentally embodied in water baptism, "gets worked out over a lifetime, whether it begins in infancy or later in life."[19]

13. Pinnock, *Most Moved Mover*, 164.
14. Pinnock, *Flame of Love*, 149.
15. Pinnock, *Most Moved Mover,* 170.
16. Pinnock, *Flame of Love*, 166.
17. Chan, *Pentecostal Theology*, 53.
18. Pinnock, *Flame of Love*, 167.
19. Pinnock, *Flame of Love*, 168.

Initiation, then, "is the beginning, not the ending."[20] Because salvation is a lifelong process, one should expect to experience moments of renewal by the Spirit (2 Tim 1:6). In his words, "renewal is not accomplished suddenly but progressively—"from glory to glory" (see 2 Cor 3:18)."[21] Often it takes time for one's "baptismal initiation to work itself out in a holy life."[22] Considering transformation comes not by "instant metamorphosis but by gradual transformation," Pinnock leaves open the possibility that conformity to Christ continues after death.[23]

Significant to Pinnock's process-oriented view of salvation is his following of Orthodoxy's distinction between "a created image" and "an acquired likeness":

> The one term speaks of a created given, the other of a potential future. It lets us view Spirit as moving humans from created image to Christlikeness. It lets us think of human beings as presently not in their final state but unfinished, needing to grow toward maturity and perfection. We do not now possess both aspects of the image of God; likeness is to be realized only in the future in communion with God, when our relationship with God and our fellows is complete.[24]

All believers are being conformed over a lifetime to the image of Christ through the Spirit.[25] One should not expect instantaneous change. Being conformed into the likeness to Christ "is a dynamic and gradual process."[26] Just as physical growth toward maturity takes time, so too does growing into the likeness of Jesus. It does not happen all at once, but it is rather oftentimes "a long, gradual journey."[27]

20. Pinnock, *Flame of Love*, 169.
21. Pinnock, *Flame of Love*, 168.
22. Pinnock, *Flame of Love*, 176.
23. Pinnock, *Flame of Love*, 179.
24. Pinnock, *Flame of Love*, 174.
25. Pinnock, "Great Jubilee," 99.
26. Pinnock, *Flame of Love*, 175.
27. Pinnock, *Flame of Love*, 176.

Instead of addressing individual categories within the topic of salvation, Pinnock thinks that "the best way to understand topics such as justification, sanctification, and the new birth is to see them as overlapping metaphors of salvation in the rich tapestry of scriptural soteriology."[28] If one must distinguish between these various components, Pinnock does so by considering justification that which points to God's acceptance of us, sanctification that which points to the process of salvation in us, and regeneration that which points to our new being in Christ.[29] However, Pinnock prefers to bring these various conceptions together within the broader category of transformation/union. Ultimately, therefore, "conformity with Christ as salvation becomes effective in this life and moves in the direction of complete renewal."[30]

In Pinnock's construction, Jesus' saving activity is pertinent to individuals, societies, and the cosmos.[31] For instance, he notes that the notion of cosmic reconciliation was a major theme in the Old Testament and was picked up in several notable places in the New Testament. Further, the sanctification of society is also something God is interested in. Though the completion of the renewal lies ahead of us, God is already working in the present to renew all things. As he sees it, "God does this primarily through Christians in their communities, living out the gospel in society and salting it as they live out of their hope and act out of their hope and act out of their love."[32] However, since we are "on the side of the future," Christians should promote policies that establish justice and peace.[33]At the same time, he is clear the kingdom cannot be brought about by our efforts, since it grounded upon gift, not achievement.

28. Pinnock and Brown, *Theological Crossfire*, 201.

29. Pinnock and Brown, *Theological Crossfire*, 201.

30. Pinnock and Brown, *Theological Crossfire*, 201.

31. Pinnock and Brown, *Theological Crossfire*, 204.

32. Pinnock and Brown, *Theological Crossfire*, 201.

33. Pinnock and Brown, *Theological Crossfire*, 204.

PARTICIPATION IN GOD

Compared to other Protestant theologians, Pinnock is unique in that he looks at salvation through the lens of the Spirit. Once again, though Pinnock makes use of the typical Western categories of justification and sanctification,[34] Pinnock focuses most intently on salvation's goal, which is "the loving embrace of God."[35] Acquittal is only the beginning of salvation, not the end. Pinnock insists that union with God is the destination. In Pinnock's opinion, Protestants have too often made justification the end-all of salvation:

> This means that the legal dimension has dominated our thinking about salvation. Being forgiven and acquitted is no doubt important. Justification is a moment in salvation, but not necessarily the central motif. Since we have been forgiven, our eyes are on the goal of union with the love of God.[36]

The ancient conception that has focused on this union dimension is the Eastern doctrine of theosis. Following Irenaeus and Athanasius, Pinnock believes that "God became man, that man might become God."[37] Put another way, salvation is not simply a matter of being pardoned, but transformed and "divinized."[38] Within this view, Christians are enabled to participate in God's divine nature (2 Pet 1:4). God desires a transforming friendship with his creatures that leads to sharing in his triune life. Salvation, then, is directed toward God's loving embrace.

But union, theosis, or divinization, as Pinnock sees it, is not some form of pantheism. God's people are enabled to participate in the divine nature in a way that conserves the differentiations between Creator and creature.[39] In other words,

34. Pinnock and Brow, *Unbounded Love*, 112–13.
35. Pinnock, *Flame of Love*, 150.
36. Pinnock, *Flame of Love*, 155.
37. Pinnock, *Flame of Love*, 154.
38. Pinnock, *Flame of Love*, 151.
39. Pinnock, *Flame of Love*, 150–51.

> United to Christ without becoming Christ, we are also united to God without becoming God. It is a personal union in which the distinction between Creator and creature is maintained. We enter the dance of the Trinity not as equals but as adopted partners. When Peter says we participate in the divine nature, he is indicating not ontological union but union in resurrected bodies. This is a personal union, not an ontological union. It does not deny the distinction between God and creature or make God the only reality.[40]

Within this conception, union with God is a state of intimacy. We are invited to participate "in this divine dance of loving communion."[41] In Pinnock's perspective, our human nature has been restored and made capable of participation in God because of Christ. The union of the two natures of Christ has made a way for his people to experience true union with God.

Following Scripture's lead, at times Pinnock uses sexual imagery to denote such intimacy. As Paul states to the Ephesians, the love of husband and wife is a signpost of the mystery of Christ's love for his people (Eph 5:29–31). Salvation is directed to a wedding (Rev 19:9). All of this implies that salvation "is more like falling in love with God" than anything else.[42] Union with God, though fully realized in the future, begins in the present through a transformative and loving friendship with God.

RELIGIOUS PLURALISM

Because God is a lover of all humanity, he desires all to be saved (1 Tim 2:4). Yet, "how is the voice of God heard outside communities where Christ is named?"[43] This question—along with others—have been raised within the contemporary theological conversation surrounding salvation, due to religious pluralism. As a result, Pinnock

40. Pinnock, *Flame of Love*, 154.
41. Pinnock, *Flame of Love*, 153.
42. Pinnock, *Flame of Love*, 156.
43. Pinnock, *Flame of Love*, 186.

considers theology to be under pressure to find a reason for its hope in the person of Jesus within the context of world religions.[44] Though in one sense, religious pluralism is not a new problem, there are various factors in the present situation that make the problem feel particularly pressing for modern, Western people.

Pinnock notes that the relativistic thinking of late modernity has fostered a new form of pluralism in which all truth claims are considered equally valid paths to a universal destination. Also, unlike in the two-third worlds for whom "pluralism is a fact of daily life," those in the West "have been culturally sheltered."[45] As such, those of us within this context are just now beginning to grapple with an interreligious environment. Due largely to these two factors, Pinnock believes that there is a great need for theology to address the challenge of religious pluralism.

Within the current theological discussion, Pinnock discerns two equal and opposite errors. One is to firmly declare that all will be saved, while the other is to say only a few will be. On Pinnock's account, those within mainline churches often fall prey to the former, while their Evangelicals counterparts succumb to the latter. As he sees it, both are mistaken. Pinnock wants to forge a way between these two dichotomies of "pluralism" and "exclusivism."[46] In response, Pinnock seeks to forge an "inclusivistic" vision that upholds "Christ as the Savior of humanity" while also affirming "God's saving presence in the wider world and in other religions."[47] He explains his position this way:

> One could say that my proposal is exclusivist in affirming a decisive redemption in Jesus Christ, although it does not deny the possible salvation of non-Christian people. Similarly, it could be called inclusivist in refusing

44. Pinnock, "Toward an Evangelical Theology," 359.

45. Pinnock, *Wideness in God's Mercy*, 9.

46. As Pinnock defines them, pluralism is the position that denies the finality of Jesus Christ and maintains the possible salvation of non-Christian people apart of Jesus, while exclusivism maintains Christ as Savior of the world but considers all other religious as total zones of darkness. See Pinnock, *Wideness in God's Mercy*, 14–15.

47. Pinnock, *Wideness in God's Mercy*, 15.

> to limit the grace of God to the confines of the church, although it hesitates to regard other religions as salvific vehicles in their own right. It might even be called pluralist insofar as it acknowledges God's gracious work in the lives of human beings everywhere and accepts real differences in what they believe, though not pluralist in the sense of eliminating the finality of Christ or falling into relativism.[48]

Pinnock does not expect his interpretation to solve all problems or answer all questions within this complex dialogue. Rather, his hope is to provide a general framework in which "a better Evangelical solution to the problem of other religions might be found."[49] As we will see, methodologically, Pinnock begins his constructive efforts christologically, by taking a fresh look at the good news of the gospel.

"Jesus, Savior of the World"

Predicated on a thorough examination of biblical texts, Pinnock concludes that God sent Jesus to be Savior of the entire world, not merely the Savior of a select few.[50] Pinnock believes that taken as a whole, Scripture reveals God desiring salvation for the whole world and the entire human race (Titus 2:11). As he puts it, "the Biblical scenario is expansive and inclusive."[51] Thus, in developing a theology of religions, one must emphasize that God's redemptive work in Christ is intended to benefit all. What is needed is a "hermeneutic of hopefulness" over and against the hardline restrictive readings that have relegated the majority of people to predestined damnation. In such theologies, only a minority of people "are the fortunate recipients of an arbitrary and unmerited divine favor."[52] Such readings of Scripture, on Pinnock's account, are entirely mistaken.

48. Pinnock, *Wideness in God's Mercy*, 15.
49. Pinnock, *Wideness in God's Mercy*, 15.
50. Pinnock, *Wideness in God's Mercy*, 47.
51. Pinnock, "Toward an Evangelical Theology," 361.
52. Pinnock, "Toward an Evangelical Theology," 361.

In emphasizing an expansive vision for salvation, Pinnock does not sacrifice a high Christology. In his mind, the Incarnation does not diminish, but rather supports one's trust in the comprehensive salvific will of God. Christ's work is cosmic in scope and not simply limited to a particular time and place.

> It is important to remember that the Logos, which was made flesh in Jesus of Nazareth, is present in the entire world and in the whole of human history. Though Jesus is Lord, we confess at the same time that the Logos is not confined to one segment of human history or one piece of world geography.[53]

Jesus' work in the world is wide and expansive. Pinnock maintains that one can hold to the universality of God's saving grace while also holding to the particularity of salvation through Christ alone. These two axioms do not stand in contradiction. The finality of Christ does not hinder the world's salvation, but rather makes it possible. In Christ, "we find the particular that functions in a saving way for the whole of our common humanity."[54]

Though Pinnock consults many Scriptures throughout his construction, he believes that Acts 17:16–34 is particularly instructive for developing a theology of religions. In his reading of the text, Paul "accepts that the Athenians are worshipping God, howbeit unknowingly."[55] Significantly, Paul was willing to grant that the Athenians were seeking God in their religious life, due to the providence of God. Pinnock notes that though the Christ event is decisive, it alone does not contain all of God's salvific activity within the whole of human history. On the contrary, we ought to follow Paul in viewing the gospel as the "fulfillment of all genuine human seeking after God."[56] Pinnock sees Paul's approach as dialectical and balanced and calls his readers to emulate it. The goal, then, is to

53. Pinnock, *Wideness in God's Mercy*, 77.

54. Pinnock, "Toward an Evangelical Theology," 362.

55. Pinnock, "Toward an Evangelical Theology," 365.

56. Pinnock, "Toward an Evangelical Theology," 365.

promote interreligious dialogue while maintaining the scriptural pronouncement that salvation is through Jesus alone.[57]

What might this imply about religions themselves and those who are a part of them? Here Pinnock proposes that religions "present us with mixed signals."[58] Religions are part of fallen human systems. They are often resistant to Christ and may be under satanic influence. Still, not all religions are opposed to Christ in the same manner. For Pinnock, "whatever truth and goodness is to be found in the religions now is evidence of God's work and not a denial of salvation through Jesus Christ."[59] God is not finished with history and continues to work within it. Whatever is good, beautiful, and true within other religions is "due to the prevenient grace of the triune God seeking sinners."[60] Further, Pinnock asserts that God judges the lost in relation to the light they have, not according to the light that did not reach them. God's judgment is wholly just. It considers "what people are conscious of, what they yearn for, what they have suffered, what they do out of love, and so forth."[61]

The Universal Spirit

There is a tension intrinsic to the Christian faith between universality and particularity. For example, Christians believe that God loves the whole world, while at the same time trusting that Jesus is the only way to God. In his approach to issues surrounding religious plurality, Pinnock holds that there must be an affirmation of both the particular and the universal, without reducing either one. Theologian Veli-Matti Kärkkäinen has rightly noted that "Pinnock started his move toward inclusivism mainly on a christological basis but then later shifted to a definite pneumatological view," without suggesting any contradiction between these two directions.[62] To-

57. Pinnock, "Toward an Evangelical Theology," 360.
58. Pinnock, "Toward an Evangelical Theology," 364.
59. Pinnock, *Wideness in God's Mercy*, 113.
60. Pinnock, *Wideness in God's Mercy*, 103.
61. Pinnock, "Toward an Evangelical Theology," 368.
62. Kärkkäinen, *Introduction*, 269.

gether, these orientations provide a way forward for Pinnock, since Jesus reveals particularity while the Spirit conveys universality.[63]

> Christ, the only mediator, sustains particularity, while Spirit, the presence of God everywhere, safeguards universality. Christ represents particularity by being the only mediator between God and humanity (1 Tim 2:5–6), while Spirit upholds universality because no soul is beyond the sphere of the Spirit's operations.[64]

Those who assume that most of humanity will be consigned to damnation, whether they hear the gospel or not, have not considered the Spirit's universal presence and workings. When considered from the standpoint of the Spirit, access to grace is less of an issue. The Spirit's cosmic activities ought to help Christian re-conceptualize the comprehensive nature of God's grace.[65] In Pinnock's vision, the categories of general and special revelation need to be reassessed in light of the Spirit's universal presence. As he sees it, we need to affirm that "there is grace in general revelation and special revelation, and both are fulfilled in Jesus Christ."[66] This suggests that there cannot be general revelation that is not at the same time potentially saving revelation.

The category of prevenient grace is central to Pinnock's construction. The Spirit is working in lives long before it can be detected. The Spirit urges and woos all people toward himself. Therefore, "because of Spirit, everyone has the possibility of encountering him—even those who have not heard of Christ may establish a relationship with God through prevenient grace."[67] Therefore, rather than stating that there is no salvation outside the church, we ought to declare that there is no salvation outside grace. This implies, then, that "salvation can be a universal possibility if we recognize the universal, loving activities of the Spirit."[68]

63. Pinnock, *Flame of Love*, 188.
64. Pinnock, *Flame of Love*, 192.
65. Pinnock, *Flame of Love*, 187.
66. Pinnock, *Flame of Love*, 194.
67. Pinnock, *Flame of Love*, 199.
68. Pinnock, *Flame of Love*, 198.

In response to such assertions, Pinnock asks whether there is a possibility that the Spirit is at work in other faiths.[69] In response, Pinnock begs the question, "why would the Spirit be working everywhere else but not here?"[70] Whatever truth lies within other religions is a result of the Spirit's work within that religious tradition. Because religions are dynamic realities that change over time, Pinnock believes that the Spirit seeks to influence them over time. Yet, "though most religions contain some truth, they also contain much that is dark and oppressive."[71] We cannot ignore error and darkness. The Holy Spirit is not the only spirit active within the religious sphere. However, regardless of the many inadequacies and distortions that are found in various religions, Pinnock is optimistic about the Spirit's missional activity within them. God does not leave himself without witness and is always pursuing the lost (Acts 14:17).

To discern the Spirit's work, then, Pinnock urges Christians to consider interreligious dialogue and comparative theology. In his mind, Christians in the past "have listened to non-Christian voices, such as Plato and Aristotle, because they thought they had truth to offer."[72] Why stop there, then? Open dialogue with other religious voices should not diminish faith commitment to Christ, but rather it should lead to hope that the Spirit will lead toward mutual enrichment. Such encounters might also provide opportunity for proclaiming Christ as well as forging greater bridges of communication. Therefore, "there is nothing to fear from interreligious dialogue."[73]

In the end, though, Pinnock believes we must say "yes and no to other religions."[74] On the one hand, Christians ought to acknowledge truth and spiritual insight within them. On the other hand, we must oppose darkness and recognize that they are lacking

69. Pinnock, *Flame of Love*, 200.
70. Pinnock, *Flame of Love*, 201.
71. Pinnock, *Flame of Love*, 206.
72. Pinnock, *Flame of Love*, 201.
73. Pinnock, *Flame of Love*, 205.
74. Pinnock, *Flame of Love*, 202.

apart from the fulfillment of Christ.[75] Yet he maintains that "one can be sensitive to the Spirit among people of other faiths without minimizing real and crucial differences between them."[76] Hence, Pinnock again emphasizes holding to the tension of "the universal operations of grace and the uniqueness of its manifestation in Jesus Christ."[77]

What does all of this suggest then about the relationship between salvation and those within other religious? Pinnock is clear: Other religions do *not* mediate Christian salvation, for Christ is the "only mediator."[78] However, he imagines people are saved according to their faith, not according to their theology. People are judged by the light they have received and how they have responded to that light. God accepted Abraham and David because of their faith, even though they were ignorant to the revelation contained within Christ. Pagans in the Old Testament, too, such as Job and Abimelech, were accepted through their faith in God, despite their lack of knowledge. Pinnock sees the case of Cornelius to be especially helpful in this regard: "God does not show favoritism but accepts men from every nation who fear him and do what is right" (Acts 10:34–35).[79]

Pinnock, then, calls for hopefulness in light of God's boundless love:

> Let us never give up hope for those who have not yet believed. For one thing, who can say what a no means? What if the gospel was heard from a drunken sailor? What if the message was distorted? What if a zealous restrictivist had portrayed God as particularly niggardly? What would a no mean? What if the no will turn into a yes by the last day? Do we have any notion how hard it must be for not-yet-Christians to extricate themselves from their own cultural- linguistic communities and become baptized Christians? How many of us had to make

75. Pinnock, *Flame of Love*, 202.
76. Pinnock, *Flame of Love*, 207.
77. Pinnock, *Flame of Love*, 202.
78. Pinnock, *Flame of Love*, 192.
79. Pinnock, *Wideness in God's Mercy*, 165.

> a costly decision like that? Let us be filled with sympathy and not at all judgmental, even toward those who have seemed to say no to Jesus until now.[80]

CONCLUSION

Pinnock believes that because God is love, the possibility of salvation—union with God—exists for *everyone*. Jesus is the Savior of the entire world, not merely the Savior of a select few. God desires that all would be saved even though some will turn away and reject God's invitation. As to be expected, Reformed Evangelical Calvinists such as John Piper, Bruce Ware, and others have taken issue with Pinnock's inclusive view of salvation.[81] Daniel Strange, too, has sought to challenge Pinnock's understanding of the scope of salvation.[82] Against Pinnock, he argues for a limited atonement, in which God's saving purposes are only intended to encompass a limited, pre-chosen group of people. In response to such challenges, I. Howard Marshall rightly notes that these Reformed Evangelicals are not just directing their critiques "against Pinnock but against all non-Reformed evangelicalism."[83] In Marshall's opinion, "the New Testament clearly teaches that the death of Christ was not limited in scope" thus, any attempt "to undermine this part of the foundation of Clark Pinnock's theological exploration is not successful, and the issues that he raises cannot be so easily avoided or regarded as improper."[84]

A more friendly critique of Pinnock's "theological inclusivism" comes a fellow inclusivist, Pentecostal theologian Amos Yong. Though sympathetic with Pinnock's work, Yong challenges Pinnock in thinking through how to better explain how the presence of the Spirit is discerned in other religious contexts.[85] Rather than under-

80. Pinnock, *Flame of Love*, 214.

81. See Piper et al., *Beyond the Bounds*; Ware, *God's Lesser Glory*.

82. Strange, *Possibility of Salvation*.

83. Marshall, "For All," 323.

84. Marshall, "For All," 346.

85. Yong, "Whither Theological Inclusivism?," 327–48; Pinnock, "Response

mining Pinnock's claim surrounding the universality of grace like the other Evangelical critics, Yong applauds Pinnock on this front but tasks him to pay more attention to empirical religions. However, other critiques of Pinnock come from theologically liberal theologians, who believe that Pinnock should consider the strengths of other pluralistic frameworks.[86]

Yet, there is still more ground to cover regarding Pinnock's understanding of salvation. As we have seen, Pinnock *does* allow for salvation outside the church due to God's boundless love. However, this does not suggest that Pinnock has a truncated view of the church. As we will see in the following chapter, Pinnock strongly believes that salvation is "historically mediated" and often "comes in the form of a new community."[87]

to Daniel Strange and Amos Yong," 349–57.

86. Pinnock and Brown, *Theological Crossfire*, 192.

87. Pinnock and Brown, *Theological Crossfire*, 198.

5

Church: Power & Presence

As Pinnock considers it, the church is the community on earth that corresponds to the fellowship within the triune life, by being a place of mutuality and self-giving.[1] As such, the church is intended to depict what God desires the world to become. While the church is the body of Christ, the fellowship of the Spirit, and even an institution, most supremely the church is the Spirit-indwelled community meant to reflect the communion and love of the Trinity to the world. As the church resounds trinitarian relations, it bears witness to the coming kingdom and announces the intended destiny of all creation. Responding to this vocation, the Spirit anointed church experiences the power and presence of God sacramentally and charismatically, for the sake of its mission.[2]

A SACRAMENTAL COMMUNITY

Pinnock believes that the church must confront the matter-Spirit dualism that is so prevalent. Though brought up in the free-church tradition, he came to recognize the value of the "physical side of being spiritual" through a fresh reading of Scripture and through

1. Pinnock, *Flame of Love*, 117.

2. Pinnock, *Flame of Love*, 119.

a growing appreciation of the Catholic, Orthodox, and Protestant traditions.[3] Since Christ is the primal sacrament or sacrament of God,[4] the church is the sacrament of Christ.[5] The church indwelled by the Spirit mediates the presence and life of God to the world. Since the "sacraments are sacred signs, made up of words and actions, employing material symbols, through which God bestows life on us by the Spirit,"[6] the term sacrament, for Pinnock, serves as a general category for created reality that is used by God to mediate his presence. The whole world, then, is God's temple. Because God is everywhere and in everything, God encounters the created world, utilizing it to magnify himself and mediate grace.

Sacraments are essential because we are fleshly beings dwelling within a material world, and therefore, material signs encourage the relationship between God and his creatures. Therefore, there is no limit to the number of sacraments; all created existence is abundantly infused with sacramental potentials. God has made his creation to reflect his beauty. If one is open to God's revelation, much of anything can mediate the sacred. The Spirit's presence pervades the universe, implying that anything can be utilized. Pinnock understands this to be supported by Scripture. For instance, the burning bush (Acts 7:30) and God speaking to Elijah through the elements of the earth (1 Kgs 19:11–12) demonstrates God's desire to facilitate his presence by way of his creation.[7]

Pinnock, then, believes that the "sacramental principle" operates not only within the church, but within the whole world, as well. This is shown in Pinnock's distinction between natural sacraments and ecclesial sacraments. Regarding ecclesial sacraments, Pinnock states that churchly activities such as singing, prayer, fellowship, and foot-washing can all be sacramental. Further, because reading Scripture mediates the Word of God, it is in a sense, sacramental. Thus, Christ's sacramental presence is with his church through

3. Pinnock, "Physical Side of Being Spiritual," 8.

4. Pinnock thinks that Karl Barth takes this to an extreme in naming Christ as the sole sacrament.

5. Pinnock, "Physical Side of Being Spiritual," 13.

6. Pinnock, "Physical Side of Being Spiritual," 13.

7. Pinnock, *Flame of Love*, 120

embodied worship. In his words, "the physical and the spiritual are not antithetical but cooperative and synergistic."[8]

Nonetheless, there are two chief sacraments of the church: baptism, which initiates people into the community, and eucharist, which renews participation in it. These two central sacraments have been present from the beginning of church life, while others have been added yet formulated in relation to these two. The sacrament of confirmation and reconciliation, for instance, are related to baptism, whereas marriage, anointing of the sick, and ordination are related to eucharist.[9] Baptism and eucharist, then, are central to the life of the church and holy "events in which God moves."[10]

As a free-church Baptist, Pinnock is unique in that he does not draw a distinct line between water baptism and Spirit baptism. He considers baptism to be the moment in which the Spirit is imparted and when believers are opened to the Spirit's gifts. Within this understanding, baptism is not merely a human response or symbolic ordinance, but instead, baptism is an act of God in which the Spirit initiates people into the community of Christ. Given the fact that when Jesus was baptized in water, he received the Spirit, we too should expect Christ to baptize us in water and Spirit. Scripture connects the coming of the Spirit with water baptism and is aligned with church tradition.[11]

Although the Spirit is given in water baptism in conjunction with faith, one can be filled with the Spirit many times in terms of appropriation. Put another way, while one does not receive the person of the Spirit more than once, the Spirit awakens one to his work and effects over a lifetime. This is especially true in the case of infant baptism. Even though Pinnock's preference is for dedication of infants and water baptism later in life, he asserts that infant baptism paired with robust confirmation could achieve similar results. This would imply that the Spirit is present within infant baptism, "with the effectiveness of it unfolding gradually as the child grows in faith

8. Pinnock, *Flame of Love*, 122.

9. Pinnock, *Flame of Love*, 124.

10. Pinnock, *Flame of Love*, 129.

11. Pinnock, *Flame of Love*, 125.

over the years."[12] However, whether one chooses infant baptism or believers baptism, Pinnock suggests that the relationship between water baptism and Spirit baptism remain. He then encourages communities to consider which danger is greatest:

> The danger of baptizing infants is that the action might be regarded as magical and the importance of faith be lost sight of. We must not rely on a ritual to save us in the absence of a call to serious discipleship. The danger of insisting on believers' baptism, on the other hand, is that we might regard the human decision so highly that we forget God's enabling grace. What about the mentally handicapped? Can God not work grace in the young and weak? Can the Spirit not anoint them? It also places the children of believers in an awkward position ecclesially.[13]

Whether a community opts for infant baptism or believers' baptism, initiation into Christ and his community looks toward a lifetime of discipleship, whomever the candidate and whatever the timing.[14]

Regarding the eucharist, the believer receives Christ in the form of bread and wine, participating in his death and resurrection. Thus, the Spirit is to be evoked upon the elements that they might become vehicles of grace. This denotes that the efficacy of the sacrament has nothing to do with any "magical" operation, but instead has everything to do with the Spirit's presence. Further, the focus should not be on the transformation of the elements, but on the Spirit's working within the whole of the ceremony. In this way, one sees Pinnock's appreciation for the Eastern churches. The believer experiences the presence of Christ through the Spirit in response to prayer. Without genuine faith, the sacrament is barren and ineffectual. God desires our participation in his coming, suggesting that one cannot neglect the preparation of people.[15] The eucharist is not merely a symbolic, memorial meal, but instead, a true occasion for the Spirit to mediate

12. Pinnock, *Flame of Love*, 126.

13. Pinnock, *Flame of Love*, 126.

14. Pinnock's ecumenical openness on baptism causes him to reject the practice of rebaptism. See Pinnock and Brow, *Unbounded Love*, 128.

15. Pinnock, "Physical Side of Being Spiritual," 17.

the presence of Christ to the participant. In this way, the eucharist is food for the spiritually hungry—true bread from heaven.

Overall, in articulating a theology of the sacraments two errors must be avoided. The first error is to overstate the objective nature of the sacraments and thus diminish the relational encounter with God. Yet an equally dangerous error is to overemphasize the importance of personal faith and consequently make the sacraments more our actions than God's. Pinnock sees the Spirit as the key to the effectiveness of the sacraments, yet also concurs with Vatican II that faith is required.[16] This two-fold emphasis upon divine initiative and human response avoids mechanical efficacy and lifts up relationality. For Pinnock, then, the solution is to understand the sacraments as a truly objective "means of grace in which the Spirit renders material things and actions graciously efficacious to faith."[17]

A CHARISMATIC COMMUNITY

Along with the sacraments, Pinnock emphasizes the necessity of the gifts of the Spirit operating within the life of the church. He states, "I would not want to see a revival of sacramentality which was not a renewal at the same time of charismaticality."[18] If the sacramental and charismatic facets of the church could be carried together as they were early in the church's history, Pinnock believes it could help facilitate the healing of divisions within the church.[19] Consequently, he deeply desires to recover the "two-dimensionality of charism and sacrament original to Christianity."[20] This should be natural given that the church is fundamentally the anointed community of the Spirit. The Spirit is active beyond traditional liturgy in healing the sick, prophecy, visions, and enthusiastic worship. Scripture attests to the fact that the church has been infused with a variety of gifts that will not be withdrawn before the End. The church—though weak in

16. Pinnock, *Flame of Love*, 123.

17. Pinnock, "Great Jubilee," 97.

18. Pinnock, "Physical Side of Being Spiritual," 14.

19. Pinnock, "Great Jubilee," 98.

20. Pinnock, *Flame of Love*, 120.

and of itself—is gifted with power by the Spirit for the sake of the world. The creative Spirit equips and energizes the church for ministry until God's objectives within history are realized.[21] Because the New Testament does not distinguish between charismatic and non-charismatic Christians, all believers need to understand themselves as filled with and gifted by the Spirit.

Pinnock seeks to confront what he sees to be the erroneous dichotomy between charisms bestowed upon ordained clergy and the laity. For Pinnock, the church is a charismatic fellowship with many giftings, "including but surpassing ordained leadership."[22] Therefore, while high church traditions have informed his sacramentality, his rootedness within the free-church tradition informs his charismatic structuring of the church. For Pinnock, every member of the body of Christ is a priest and minister, gifted for the greater good of the community.[23] In the history of the church, needed rejuvenation at times has been slowed by clericalism and control, snuffing out "charismatic structures and gifts."[24]

However, Pinnock does not imply that officeholders are not needed. For there must be a dialectic of freedom and order—office alongside charism. This suggests neither a "supercharged church without discipline nor a lifeless church without Spirit."[25] Instead, there is a tension between charism and institution. This is achieved by holding up discerning officeholders who seek to nurture the gifts of the community, utilizing them for the common good.[26] Officeholders, then, should be aware of the church's historical inclination toward rigidity. Pinnock as a rule believes that embracing a charismatic structuring assists in the community's long-term health and vitality.

And since the New Testament does not prescribe official and formal organizing structures, the church should embrace practical,

21. Pinnock, *Flame of Love*, 130.

22. Pinnock, *Flame of Love*, 131.

23. Pinnock, "Church in the Power," 160.

24. Pinnock, "Church in the Power," 159.

25. Pinnock, *Flame of Love*, 140.

26. Pinnock, *Flame of Love*, 140.

culturally sustainable, and temporally adaptable forms, which in Pinnock's mind, best serves the work of the Kingdom.[27] It is vital that communities give the Spirit priority over structures and offices, even though they too are given by the Spirit for the sake of the church.[28] One of Pinnock's central concerns, then, is to help the church avoid quenching the Spirit. This is one element that he seeks to applaud within Pentecostalism. Naturally, Pentecostals promote a lively faith in the Spirit, providing believers with occasions to participate in the life of the body through the gifts with which the Spirit equips them.[29]

As the early church practiced and contemporary Pentecostalism has revived, the Christian experience should include an energetic approach to faith that emphasizes an encounter with God. The Spirit acts beyond sacramental rites in and through ecstatic giftings. In particular, Pinnock observes three gifts that he imagines the church ought to recover.[30] First, the church should embrace the gift of prophecy, since Paul saw it is the most important gift in a community (1 Cor 14:1). Like tongues—prophecy is a gift that arises from listening to and speaking by the Spirit. Teachers are of vital importance to the church, but the role of the prophet must be revived. Prophecy cannot be equated with teaching. Inspired speech must once again be embraced. Yet, there must be discernment and testing of prophetic utterances. We cannot quench the Spirit, but we must also test everything (1 Thess 5:19–21). In the end, the fear of false prophets must not prevent us from hearing from God and promoting the role of prophecy.

Healing prayer, too, as seen in the ministry of Jesus and the early church is a practice in need of retrieval. Here the sacramental and charismatic meet. When we anoint the sick with oil, the Spirit makes himself present sacramentality and charismatically. Yet, embracing divine healing does not imply a rejection of medical science. In Pinnock's own words, "skill in medicine is a creational charism."[31] Because the Spirit of the church is also the Spirit of

27. Pinnock, "Church in the Power ," 162.

28. Pinnock, "Church in the Power," 162.

29. Pinnock, "Church in the Power," 157.

30. Pinnock, *Flame of Love*, 134–36.

31. Pinnock, *Flame of Love*, 135.

creation, healing prayers of the faithful summon the power of healing at work in creation. All creation is destined toward resurrection, and healing is at most a "temporary stop-gap."[32] Until resurrection comes in full, sickness and death are inevitable. Still, God seeks to relieve suffering and grant foretastes of the coming cosmic healing here and now. Since God maintains the constancy of the universe, he may not interfere as often as we might wish. Thus, prayers for healing must embrace a posture of surrender and trust, recognizing God's freedom, while also asking for needs confidently.

Exorcism and discerning of spirits are other giftings of the Spirit for the church that need reconsidering. Pinnock recognizes that at times superstition have accompanied such practices. However, he argues that believers cannot make the equal mistake in diminishing the struggle between Christ's kingdom and the kingdom of darkness. Just as God has granted freedom to humanity and his creation, freedom has—by extension—also been granted to demonic entities.[33] Therefore, because God's authority is contested by the demonic powers, deliverance is a necessary and important ministry of the church. Following the ministry of Jesus, the church has been granted the responsibility of pushing back against the darkness. With these affirmations in mind, though, Pinnock seeks to balance the perspective by asserting that the typical categories of "natural" and "supernatural" needs revisioning. God is both active in creation *and* redemption. Therefore, gifts of the Spirit "can animate natural capacities and may not be foreign to nature as created by God."[34] In the case of discerning of spirits, then, psychology and exorcism are not antithetical, but should work together.

Pinnock, then, urges communities to generate an openness to the move of the Spirit, while at the same time, recognizing and respecting God's freedom to be present as he wills, "on a spectrum from ordinary to extraordinary ways."[35] Just as in the case of Jesus' ministry in Nazareth, our limited expectations and scorning of the

32. Pinnock, *Flame of Love*, 135.

33. Pinnock, "Evangelical Theology after Darwin," 107.

34. Pinnock, *Flame of Love*, 137.

35. Pinnock, *Flame of Love*, 137.

miraculous can limit God's liberty to act. On this point, Pinnock exhorts his readers: "Let us ask God to disturb our tranquility so that he may surprise, refresh, empower us."[36] The church must allow God to loosen us in order to witness the potentials of new creation. In opening ourselves up to God afresh, he can renew our baptism and release its latent possibilities in the Spirit.

However, Pinnock wisely warns against regularizing a release of Easter life.[37] Since the way to Easter is only through Gethsemane, Golgotha, and Good Friday, believers should stamp out all hints of triumphalism.[38] He suggests that to focus solely on mountain-top encounters is disingenuous—and even dangerous—for this is not reflective of the life of Jesus Christ. The life of the Spirit-anointed Jesus was marked by deep suffering, too.[39] This means that the Spirit-anointed church is often led *through* difficulties rather than simply being led *from* them. The sustaining activity and presence of God through difficulty can provide meaning otherwise impossible. Victory is not the whole story, for believers will also encounter the dark night of the soul. There is a tension between suffering and victory. Nonetheless, whether in pain or triumph, the church ought to seek the reality of Pentecost because the power and presence given to the church sacramentally and charismatically is not granted for its own sake, but for the sake of mission.[40]

A MISSIONAL COMMUNITY

The Spirit's presence through sacrament and charism, in Pinnock's mind, is gifted by God to empower the church to join in his mission in healing the whole creation and making all things new.[41] The church was created to enable witnesses of God's kingdom to get caught up in the transformation of all things. Mystical ecstasy,

36. Pinnock, *Flame of Love*, 137–38.
37. Pinnock, *Flame of Love*, 129.
38. Pinnock, "Church in the Power," 159.
39. Pinnock, "Church in the Power," 158.
40. Pinnock, *Flame of Love*, 141.
41. Pinnock, *Flame of Love*, 142.

for instance, is not an end to itself, but finds its fulfillment in the renovation of the world. Like Jesus, the church exists not for its own sake, but for the sake of others. For Pinnock, too often the church has forgotten its vocation to be the continuance of Jesus' own ministry through the Spirit. He seeks to remind the church that our own baptism in the Spirit is an extension of Jesus' baptism, making our mission a continuation of his mission.[42]

This mission, therefore, is not our doing and is not built upon human effort. Instead, "it is God's mission, and we are being caught up in it."[43] The birth of the church at Pentecost serves as a reminder that the "Spirit is the power behind mission, and the church is an instrument of it, not its initiator."[44] The Spirit acts preveniently and then draws the community toward participating in God's purposes. This suggests that the mission of sharing the gospel is not dependent upon human persuasion, willpower, or force, but on the power of God. And this power equips us to participate in his mission of sharing the gospel with others. Thus, election is not simply concerned with privilege, but also with responsibility and vocation.

Further, the community is marked by ways of being in the world that are distinctive. Individuals within the church are called to inhabit lives that prefigure new creation so that the world is moved by the Spirit into the life of Christ. Otherwise, the salt loses its taste and adapts to the world. Thus, embracing a lifestyle that conforms to the ethics of Christ is in and of itself missional. In this way, the loss of interest in discipleship has negatively impacted the church's mission. Without becoming a spiritually formed disciple of Christ, embodying a new order in the world is unfeasible.[45]

The mission of God in the world also goes beyond sharing the gospel, for the goal of God's mission is concerned with holistic world transformation. Not only does the church seek to proclaim good news, but also seeks to demonstrate it by identifying with pain, building community, sharing resources, and extending

42. Pinnock, *Flame of Love*, 144.

43. Pinnock, *Flame of Love*, 145.

44. Pinnock, *Flame of Love*, 142.

45. Pinnock, *Flame of Love*, 142.

forgiveness.[46] It involves both pronouncing and exhibiting the gospel. We cannot love our neighbor without being concerned about our neighbor's lack. By being a sacrament in the world, the church meets tangible needs through deeds of love. The posture of the church is that of a servant, following the sacrificial path of Christ. In this way, the message of Jesus is materialized in the world.

Ultimately, focusing solely on the salvation of "souls" falls short of participating in God's mission, for we look also for the redemption of all creation.[47] God's mission is holistic and seeks to heal all sin, both individual and societal. Pinnock states it this way:

> Mission is holistic because sin is more than personal infraction. Sin affects the structures of the world, and we oppose sin in all its manifestations, including our own complicity in what is wrong. Conversion points, then, not only to individual change but beyond to the coming transformation of the world. Since we are creatures in society and in a world, God wants to renew both us and our created context. If God did not intend that, he would be tackling half the problem. Social sanctification and cosmic renewal are ultimately part of God's plan.[48]

This "social sanctification and cosmic renewal" take place through the people of God becoming a catalyst for societal integrity. Yet, it is crucial to wait on and follow the Spirit in our responses, for without the anointing and empowerment of God, the church is powerless to enact such change. The church cannot simply respond pragmatically or ideologically since mission is not merely social work, but actions produced and empowered by God.[49] Through the gifting of God's people, the church is able to express its missionary and compassionate heart. Therefore, the community of God ought to continue to embody Jesus' mission to the whole created order both sharing and embodying the gospel.

46. Pinnock, *Flame of Love*, 143.
47. Pinnock, *Flame of Love*, 143.
48. Pinnock, *Flame of Love*, 146.
49. Pinnock, *Flame of Love*, 145.

CONCLUSION

The church, as Pinnock understands it, is anointed by the Spirit's presence for the sake of its mission. Though coming from a free-church, Baptist background, Pinnock lifts up the Spirit's work in the sacraments due to his reading of Scripture, the weight of tradition, but also "a sense of liturgical barrenness" in Evangelical churches.[50] But Pinnock also underscores the church's access to charismatic power. In his own words, "I desire to recapture the situation of the early period as I understand it, when churches were both sacramental and charismatic."[51] Also, his view of the church's mission is quite comprehensive. He believes that God is concerned "for the whole creation—for evangelization, justice and healing."[52] Therefore, Pinnock's constructions are very ecumenically formed.

Pentecostal theologian Frank Macchia appreciates Pinnock's emphasis upon the charismatic gifts but argues that "there are people from the free churches who would feel quite uneasy with Pinnock's sacramental understanding of the Spirit's salvific work in the church."[53] While also appreciating Pinnock's emphasis upon the charismatic gifts, Pentecostal theologian Terry Cross, too, believes Pinnock is mistaken to consider water baptism and Spirit baptism to be "one and the same event."[54] However, one might imagine "high church" theologians pushing back in the opposite direction. Pinnock's emphasis upon the charismatic gifts, his refusal to standardize infant baptism, and his severe criticisms of clericalism would seem problematic to other theologians in different traditions. Yet, this is to be expected considering Pinnock is intentionally "committed to being ecumenical, drawing on insights . . . from many traditions."[55]

50. Pinnock, *Flame of Love*, 240.
51. Pinnock, "Bridge," 52.
52. Pinnock, *Flame of Love*, 240.
53. Macchia, "Tradition and the *Novum*," 44.
54. Cross, "Critical Review," 23.
55. Pinnock, *Flame of Love*, 238.

6

Hope: Finality Revisited

SINCE HISTORY IS THE working out of God's purposes, there is great reason to hope in the future. In fact, all people are created *to* hope. Eschatology, then, is not "an obscure area of doctrine" but a practical one, related to the everyday human experience.[1] Because of God's gracious love, this hope has been universalized and made available to all. Still, God will not coerce anyone to love him. God's decision to not overrule the prospect of human rejection exposes the value he places on freedom. Yet, this does not imply that only a few will be saved, for God has made salvation accessible to every person in all places and times. As Terry Cross puts it, Pinnock is a "grace-filled optimist."[2] Taken together, this indicates that there are two mistakes we must avoid within a doctrine of hope: "one is to say dogmatically that all will be saved, and the other is to say that only a few will be."[3] Here Pinnock proposes fresh ways of thinking about these issues in light of God's universal love and relationality.[4]

1. Pinnock and Brown, *Theological Crossfire*, 284.

2. Cross, "Critical Review," 26.

3. Pinnock, *Flame of Love*, 190.

4. In recounting his theological "pilgrimage," Pinnock states that he experienced a "paradigm shift" in his hermeneutical and theological lens that enabled him to "read the Bible from a different point of view, one that I believe is more truly evangelical and less rationalistic." As such, he began looking at many theological issues differently including eschatology. See Pinnock, "From

RESURRECTION AND NEW CREATION

Pinnock insists that Christian hope is rooted in the resurrection of the body, not the preservation of disembodied souls.[5] The bodily resurrection of Jesus signals the opening of a new order and future for his people. Death does not have the final word. Since the "goal of salvation is union with Christ," the process of abidance that starts in this age will be completed in "the new creation, when the dead are raised incorruptible and life is renewed in totality."[6] And as Pinnock understands it, resurrection of the human takes place within the context of a resurrected cosmos. In fact, "all history is moving toward the goal of a restored and glorified universe."[7] Yes, humanity will be resurrected, but this does not preclude God renewing all things. Even though Christians often speak of going to heaven, this is not the way Scripture describes the life beyond. Rather, Scripture talks of the new heaven and new earth, a transformed and perfected universe. When God brings things into the new order, God will be "all in all" (1 Cor 15:28). Creation will have been set free from its bondage and partake in humanity's freedom (Rom 8:21).[8]

A renewed and restored created order indicates continuity between this life and the next. God, then, will "carry over" the achievements of humanity into the new creation.[9] However, the bridge between now and then can only be overcome by God's own action, suggesting a fresh creative act. Thus, "we might say that there will be material continuity of some kind, but we cannot say exactly what kind."[10] In the meantime, Pinnock believes we can conceive of the splendor of God's future by attending to the imagery of it given in Scripture. The symbols of gold, crowns, and pearls, for example, inform us of the beauty and brilliance that will be encountered. While the reality will surpass all our imaginings, "the symbols give us an

---

Augustine to Arminius," 21.

5. Pinnock and Brow, *Unbounded Love*, 41.

6. Pinnock, *Flame of Love*, 181.

7. Pinnock and Brown, *Theological Crossfire*, 223.

8. Pinnock, *Flame of Love*, 181.

9. Pinnock and Brown, *Theological Crossfire*, 225.

10. Pinnock and Brow, *Unbounded Love*, 42.

inkling."[11] Above all, we know that such an existence will be imbued with the presence of God. Pinnock states:

> We would expect glorious worship such as we have never known. We can be sure that evil, death, sorrow, and Satan will not be there. We know that sin will be removed, and love will govern existence and all its aspects. There will be true community, perfect oneness with others. And we expect it to be a place of activity, not boring inactivity. There will still be dynamism, change, and progress. From one point of view we can speak of eternal rest, but I think we can speak also of eternal activity.[12]

Such a reality is the basis of Christian hope.

A world marked by such evil and suffering is only intelligible if such a future exists.[13] Although the believer is able to experience foretastes of that future glory here and now, much of our current existence is marked by difficulty and loss. The future glory, then, will outweigh all hardship and right all wrongs. Christian hope assures us that "human existence is not a limitless tragedy but is destined for a good fulfillment beyond death."[14] Through Christ's death and resurrection, Jesus has brought forth a new order and assured us of its future consummation. In the meantime, through the ministry of the Spirit, we can receive glimpses of this glorious future. We, along with the rest of creation, sense the birth pangs of such newness.[15] This future allows us to live in hope amid tragedy, trusting in God's future of love and fulfillment.

Living in Hope

"Reality is expressive of God's purposive activity, as created, as providentially ordered, and as moving toward a goal beyond its present

11. Pinnock and Brow, *Unbounded Love*, 41.
12. Pinnock and Brown, *Theological Crossfire*, 225.
13. Pinnock and Brown, *Theological Crossfire*, 224.
14. Pinnock and Brow, *Unbounded Love*, 39.
15. Pinnock and Brow, *Unbounded Love*, 44.

condition."[16] In making this claim, Pinnock builds upon his conviction that God acts with purpose and realizes his goals through history. Of course, this implies that life is filled with meaning. In Pinnock's vision, Christian hope is realized by trusting in God to bring creation in alignment with his purposes over time. This does not indicate, however, that we can apprehend exactly how this is taking place. Instead:

> Our claim to know what God is doing comes through revelation on the basis of God's disclosure of his purpose to us through Jesus Christ. As Paul puts it, "God has made known his hidden purpose to us (cf. Eph 1:9–10 RSV). So this is an insight not gained scientifically but theologically. It is faith knowledge, and the basis on which we are able to confess that history is full of redemptive purposes. Jesus Christ is the one who makes it possible for us to see history as a theater of God's action and hope for the realization of his intentions.[17]

We must trust that God is working out his purposes in life's events, even when it does not appear that he is.

Often, we are not able to astutely perceive God's providential activity in the world and in our lives. Still, God's self-revelation in Christ releases us to live in hope. This revelation frees us from fear and introduces us to true faith. As Pinnock puts it, Christian hope is rooted in the promise that "creation is going to become the kingdom of God and embody the reality that was revealed in and inaugurated by the coming of Jesus."[18] However, contemporary thought poses difficulties to this way of viewing the world. Rather than God being the primary agent working within history, we often envision humanity as the maker of history. Future redemption becomes humanity's unaided project. Within this framework, human accomplishment and progress are the catalysts toward a newfound social order. Pinnock calls this "eschatology without God."[19] This

16. Pinnock and Brown, *Theological Crossfire*, 215.
17. Pinnock and Brown, *Theological Crossfire*, 217.
18. Pinnock and Brown, *Theological Crossfire*, 218.
19. Pinnock and Brown, *Theological Crossfire*, 221.

vision of the world is determined upon human accomplishment, exclusive of any support from God's will. As should be expected, Pinnock rejects this human-centered eschatology.

However, as we should expect, this does not suggest that Pinnock believes all human effort is meaningless. In fact, Pinnock sees humanity "going together through life and deciding with [God] what its course shall be."[20] Through our partnering with God, the Kingdom can be "embodied in actual social structures as well as in the lives of individuals,"[21] here and now. But Pinnock is quick to emphasize that it is not our effort alone that brings about the Kingdom. Instead, its full realization "God will bring about."[22] God has chosen to work with us to bear witness to his work in the world, yet our hope is that he is going to bring it to completion. In the meantime, rather than wasting time looking at biblical prophecy "as bits of information or as pieces of a puzzle to be fitted together,"[23] we instead ought to live proclaiming and embodying the hope of Christ to the world.

DIVINE JUDGMENT

Pinnock envisions God's judgment as "caring love."[24] How might this be? Essential to this conception is Pinnock's understanding of the relationship between God's love and God's wrath. Too often God's wrath is severed from God's love, which creates an unfortunate "split in God."[25] This is a mistake since God does not have a will that seeks to save, and another will that seeks to condemn. Rather, God wants to have mercy on all, which means that "God's wrath is in the service of his love."[26]

As we outlined earlier (chapter 1), Pinnock never tires of reminding his readers that God *is* love. He is not wrath. God's love is

20. Pinnock, *Most Moved Mover*, 176.
21. Pinnock and Brown, *Theological Crossfire*, 222.
22. Pinnock and Brown, *Theological Crossfire*, 222.
23. Pinnock and Brown, *Theological Crossfire*, 223.
24. Pinnock and Brow, *Unbounded Love*, 67.
25. Pinnock and Brow, *Unbounded Love*, 68.
26. Pinnock and Brow, *Unbounded Love*, 68.

eternal, while his wrath is not.[27] God's wrath toward sin cannot be understood outside of his love for sinners. Pinnock puts it this way: "God's wrath is not a fundamental disposition inherent in God's nature but a reaction that God experiences because of his love when he is confronted by sin."[28] God is a true lover which means that wrathful judgments are aimed to lead humanity toward repentance and mercy. In relation to eschatology, judgments prior to the final judgment are not meant to be the final word. They are meant to "warn and deter, heal and restore."[29] Rather than serving as evidence that God does not love, they are in fact proof that he does!

Therefore, God's judgments must be understood within the context of his salvific objectives. Pinnock urges his readers to reconsider understanding God as a judge within the context of a family rather than a courtroom. But what does it mean to say our Father is a judge? As Pinnock envisions it, "the Judge is our Savior, one who comes to our rescue and delivers us. God accuses us and exposes sin—but only to defeat evil in us."[30] God as our divine parent desires to heal his broken and estranged children. Without exception, his longing is that all would turn to him to be restored and transformed into the image of his Son. In this family paradigm, God's judgment is within the context of a loving parent encouraging and assisting his children in becoming loving.

Judgments of God, then, are meant to warn, correct, and teach so that people may turn toward him, and as a result, flourish. Judgment means that wrongs are going to be set right and "suffering will give way to fullness of life."[31] Pinnock, again, hopes to set justification within a relational paradigm: "Much more than acquittal, justification is a rectification of our relationship with him."[32] As we see

27. Or stated another way, "wrath happens, but it does not abide." See Pinnock and Brow, *Unbounded Love*, 69.

28. Pinnock and Brow, *Unbounded Love*, 69. Or as he puts it: "Wrath is frustrated anger of a disappointed lover, not of an unappeased deity or angry judge." Pinnock, *Wideness in God's Mercy*, 180.

29. Pinnock and Brow, *Unbounded Love*, 69.

30. Pinnock and Brow, *Unbounded Love*, 73.

31. Pinnock, *Wideness in God's Mercy*, 152.

32. Pinnock and Brow, *Unbounded Love*, 72.

in Scripture, God judges individuals and nations, but his judging is gracious and forgiving. Indeed, God "cares, protects, defends, frees, intervenes, fights for, sends into exile, brings back from exile, but all the while keeps on loving us and wants never to exclude anyone, even though some many exclude themselves."[33]

Although God's judgment is aimed to set humanity free, because God respects humanity's freedom, he will never coerce or force one to accept mercy. If God had his way, "all his judgments would be penultimate, and everyone would be saved."[34] But not everyone will accept his mercy. Thus, in Pinnock's formulation, "only when judgments fail to provoke repentance do they provoke eschatological wrath. Only when the final no is rendered does God close the books on the impenitent (Rom 2:5). Before that, they remain open."[35] So while God's judgments are meant to urge people toward reconciliation, in the end, not even God can force a free response of love.

THE PROBLEM OF HELL

As Pinnock envisions it, hell is an "unquestioned reality, plainly announced in the biblical witness, but its precise nature"—traditionally outlined—"is problematic."[36] He insists that hell as eternal conscious torment is both "morally intolerable" and "biblically unnecessary."[37] The idea that God endlessly tortures sinners and whose torments are supposed to delight the hearts of believers of heaven is deeply troublesome. In response to this view, Pinnock raises the question: "How could a resurrected person burn physically and suffer psychologically forever without being materially consumed or ever losing consciousness?"[38] Augustine's response to this question—that God employs "his power to perform miracles" to keep the wicked alive and conscious to be eternally tortured—is

33. Pinnock and Brow, *Unbounded Love*, 77.
34. Pinnock and Brow, *Unbounded Love*, 70.
35. Pinnock and Brow, *Unbounded Love*, 70.
36. Pinnock, "Conditional View," 135.
37. Pinnock and Brown, *Theological Crossfire*, 226.
38. Pinnock, "Destruction of the Finally Impenitent," 244.

most disturbing to Pinnock.[39] This doctrine, coupled with the belief of double predestination, makes God out to be a moral monster.[40] He is left wondering how this doctrine can be "reconciled with the revelation of God in the face of Jesus Christ."[41]

Pinnock admits that he is "disturbed" by this doctrine and realizes that he may be "playing into the hands" of his critics by such an admission.[42] He recognizes that some will accuse him of sentimentality or a subjective sense of righteous appall. Yet, he states that: "if it is sentimentality which drives me, what drives my opponent? Is it hardheartedness and the desire for eternal retribution?"[43] Pinnock states that he will not "pretend" to be impartial:

> Let me say at the outset that I consider the concept of hell as endless torment in body and mind an outrageous doctrine, a theological and moral enormity, a bad doctrine of the tradition which needs to be changed. How can Christians possibly project a deity of such cruelty and vindictiveness whose ways include inflicting everlasting torture upon his creatures, however sinful they may have been? Surely a God who would do such a thing is more nearly like Satan than like God, at least by any ordinary moral standards, and by the gospel itself.[44]

39. Pinnock also references Jonathan Edwards' (in)famous sermon "Sinners in the Hands of an Angry God" as another example of theological literature that paints a morally intolerable view of God in relation to hell.

40. Traditionally understood, "we are asked to believe that God endlessly tortures sinners by the million, sinners who perish because the Father has decided not to elect them to salvation, though he could have done so." Pinnock, "Conditional View," 136.

41. Pinnock, "Destruction of the Finally Impenitent," 245.

42. Pinnock, "Destruction of the Finally Impenitent," 246. Pinnock admits that he began to doubt the traditional doctrine based on moral intuition rather than doubting its biblical status. However, this caused him to once again, reconsider the biblical evidence and as a result "found more substantive ground in the biblical language and imagery about the Judgment of the wicked, which predominantly conveys the idea of Destruction." See Pinnock and Brown, *Theological Crossfire*, 230.

43. Pinnock, "Destruction of the Finally Impenitent," 246. Here Pinnock acknowledges that all people are *interested* interpreters of Scripture.

44. Pinnock, "Destruction of the Finally Impenitent," 247.

The trouble, for Pinnock, is the disjunction between the traditional conception of hell with the gospel revealed in and by Jesus.[45]

Pinnock wishes to show that the solution is *not* found in putting forward a doctrine of hell that simply softens the concept by making hell a timeless state or removing physical suffering. Pinnock considers C. S. Lewis' attempt to redefine hell in *The Great Divorce* as one example.[46] Such attempts seek only to dampen the moral revulsion. What is needed, rather, is to reconceptualize the nature of hell based on an alternate reading of Scripture that emphasizes both God's desire of salvation for all and human freedom.

Rejecting Love

"God's love is offered to all, and hell is not a contradiction of that. Hell exists because love can be rejected."[47] These words reveal that crucial to Pinnock's understanding of hell is his understanding of the universality of salvation and libertarian free will. The only reason people will be in hell is because they choose it. Hell is a reality for those who endure in "faithlessness and lovelessness."[48] No one is sent to hell against their will: "Although God may sentence a sinner to condemnation, it is the sinner who freely chooses hell. Hell is not the prison from which people are longing to be freed, but a sit-in where sinners have barricaded themselves in to keep God out."[49] Because love cannot be coerced and therefore must be chosen, people are able to reject God's free offer of love. Hell arises because love can be denied:

45. For example, Pinnock asks, "Would God who tells us to love our enemies be intending to wreak vengeance on his enemies for all eternity?" See Pinnock, "Conditional View," 140.

46. Pinnock believes the problem with Lewis' view is that "by sheer speculation the biblical warnings are emasculated, and the moral problem dealt with by fancy footwork devoid of exegesis." Pinnock, "Destruction of the Finally Impenitent," 254.

47. Pinnock and Brow, *Unbounded Love*, 89.

48. Pinnock *Flame of Love*, 212.

49. Pinnock, *Wideness in God's Mercy*, 180.

> God loves the ungodly, even those who reject him finally. He does not choose to break relations with them, though they may have broken relations with him. Hell is a possibility that arises from the human side, out of rebellion and obduracy. It exists for sinners who, though forgiven, steadfastly reject their acceptance by God.[50]

As we should expect from Pinnock, the emphasis is laid upon humanity's rejection of God, rather than God's rejection of humanity.

Surely Christ died for all people, including the ungodly. And though some might think this would suggest salvation of all, Pinnock sees "the Bible's repeated warnings of final loss at the Great Judgment" as a problem to such reasoning, even if he wishes it were true, himself.[51] Jesus' warnings of final rejection and separation prevent Pinnock from entertaining universal salvation. In addition to the difficulties biblically, Christian universalism suggests that God achieves salvation for all by overpowering people's resistance and/or by "wearing them down."[52] This is problematic for the way that Pinnock sees the synergetic relationship between divine and human freedom. Not even God can force humanity to accept his love.

However, Pinnock does admit to understanding why some, when confronted with the choice between hell as eternal conscious damnation and universal salvation, would choose the latter. Without another option on the theological table, Pinnock believes that "universalism will become practically irresistible in its appeal to sensitive Christians."[53] In his mind, then, there is a great need for a third option that takes both Scripture and God's morality seriously.

Destruction of the Wicked

If everlasting conscious torment and universalism are both mistaken, what is the alternative? For Pinnock, there is a "third possibility." In Pinnock's account, "God does not raise the wicked in order to

50. Pinnock and Brow, *Unbounded Love*, 88.

51. Pinnock, "Fire, Then Nothing," 40.

52. Pinnock and Brow, *Unbounded Love*, 87.

53. Pinnock, "Fire, Then Nothing," 40.

torture them consciously forever, but rather to declare his judgment upon the wicked and to condemn them to extinction, which is the second death (Rev 20:11–15)."[54] Therefore, the fire of hell does not torment, but consumes. Pinnock's view, sometimes called annihilationism or conditional immortality, indicates that immortality is gifted to the righteous, but not the wicked. But how does this view square away with the biblical text?

According to Pinnock, Scripture gives a strong impression regarding the nature of hell as "final, irreversible destruction."[55] Often it speaks of death, destruction, and perishment when discussing the fate of unrepentant sinners. In addition to many Old Testament passages,[56] Jesus spoke of God's judgment as destruction when he spoke of God's power to destroy both body and soul in hell (Matt 10:28).[57] In fact, the rest of the New Testament writers speak of everlasting destruction of the unrepentant.[58] As Paul stated to the Romans, the wages of sin is death (Rom 6:3). Therefore, Pinnock argues that "throughout its pages, following the Old Testament lead, the New Testament employs images of death, perishing, destruction, and corruption to describe the end of the wicked."[59] By providing a scriptural basis, Pinnock seeks to demonstrate scriptural explanations for holding to the annihilationist view.

However, what might we make of the texts that have been understood to support eternal conscious torment? Pinnock responds by first stating that such texts are very few in number. Second, he deals with these "difficult texts" by affirming that they can read a multiplicity of ways.[60] Even so, why have these "difficult texts" not been read this way before? The answer for Pinnock lies in the fact that the

54. Pinnock, "Fire, Then Nothing," 40.

55. Pinnock, "Conditional View," 144.

56. For two examples, Pinnock cites Ps 37:2, 9–10, 20, 38; and Mal 4:1–2.

57. For support, Pinnock also cites Jesus' sayings in Matt 3:10, 12; 5:30; 13:30, 42, 49–50.

58. Pinnock points to 2 Thess 1:9; Gal 6:8; 1 Cor 3:17; Phil 1:28; 3:19; Rom 1:32, 6:23; 2 Pet 2:1–6, 36–37; Heb 10:39; Jude 7; Rev 20:14–15.

59. Pinnock, "Conditional View," 146.

60. For example, he mentions Mark 9:48; Matt 25:46; Luke 16:23; Rev 14:11; 20:10. See Pinnock, "Destruction of the Finally Impenitent," 256–57.

Hellenistic belief of the immortality of the soul crept into Christian theology early in its history and has since served an interpretive grid. In his own words, "the real basis of the traditional view of the nature of hell is not the Bible's talk of the wicked perishing but an unbiblical anthropology that is read into the text."[61] Unfortunately, in much of Christian thinking, the immortality of the soul has been presupposed and thus, has skewed the way these texts have been read. Pinnock cites major figures such as Augustine, Aquinas, and Calvin as examples of interpreters who assumed Plato's view that the soul is metaphysically immortal. However, when one dispenses with this conception foreign to the biblical text, it becomes clearer that in Scripture, "eternal life is a gift and not a natural possession."[62] Therefore, in this case, the Bible must be read "literally":[63] God created humans as mortals, though salvation in Christ gifts humans with everlasting life.

Pinnock wishes to demonstrate that annihilationism not only makes sense scripturally, but also better affirms God's morality and justice. God loved and died for the whole world. Those who respond to his free invitation are gifted with eternal life (John 3:16). Those who reject the invitation are simply punished through extinction. In Pinnock's view, this view of hell passes "the moral test without sacrificing biblical fidelity."[64] Further, not only does this conception of hell make more sense morally, but also makes better sense from a justice standpoint: finite sins are not punished in infinity—like in the traditional view—but nor are they overlooked and overcome through coercion, such is the case in forms of universalism. Pinnock believes that the final destruction of the wicked also resolves a cosmological dualism. Metaphysically, annihilationism is more appealing than the traditional view since "heaven and hell just go on existing alongside each other forever."[65] In light of Paul's statements that God will be "all in all" (1 Cor 15:28), it is difficult to assert that in the new creation there will still be a section of unredeemed

61. Pinnock, "Conditional View," 147

62. Pinnock and Brown, *Theological Crossfire*, 226.

63. Pinnock, "Conditional View," 147.

64. Pinnock, "Conditional View," 151.

65. Pinnock, "Destruction of the Finally Impenitent," 255.

reality. For Pinnock, the victory of Christ must mean that the only thing that remains in the new creation is "light and love."[66]

Still, even though Pinnock finds everlasting conscious torment wanting in many ways, he also accepts that "the Bible is reserved about giving us detailed information about heaven or hell, so we should try not to be too dogmatic or harsh with one another."[67] Pinnock's closing tone is similar to fellow annihilationist John Stott's when he states:

> I do not dogmatize about the position to which I have come. I hold it tentatively. But I do plead for frank dialogue among evangelicals based on Scripture. I also believe that the ultimate annihilation of the wicked should at least be accepted as a legitimate biblically founded alternative to eternal conscious torment.[68]

Like Stott, Pinnock asks his readers to embrace eschatological humility. Pinnock also seeks to put forward another way of envisioning the nature of hell that is scripturally, morally, justly, and metaphysically robust, providing a third possibility for Christians.

CONCLUSION

What can we say about hope? In Pinnock's rendering, hope is nothing less than God being "all in all" (1 Cor 15:28) in the End. Christian hope is rooted in the promise that God will make "all things new" (Rev 21:5). Pinnock believes that those who have responded to God's free love will partake in the reconciliation of all things. However, those who resist God until the End will not partake in eternal life. God will allow them to finally perish. Though Pinnock's view of hell, often called "annihilationism" or "conditional immortality," has grown in popularity among Evangelicals,[69] the view is still not without its critics.

66. Pinnock, "Conditional View," 147.

67. Pinnock, "Destruction of the Finally Impenitent," 258.

68. Edwards and Stott, *Essentials*, 319–20.

69. Notable Evangelical theologians such as John Stackhouse and Preston Sprinkle embracing annihilationism as a position are both examples of the

For instance, in response to Pinnock's presentation of the "conditional view," theologians John Walvoord (literal view), William Crocket (metaphorical view), and Zachary Hayes (purgatorial view) all responded critically to Pinnock's proposal.[70] Walvoord states that Pinnock's version of annihilationism is "wishful thinking" that comes from the desire "to escape the problem of hell." Despite Pinnock's engagement with Scripture, Walvoord concludes that Pinnock denies "what the Bible teaches" regarding hell.[71] Crocket, on the other hand, believes that Pinnock's "defense of annihilationism is interesting and contains many good points,"[72] but in the end, he believes Pinnock succumbs to "emotionally charged arguments designed to sweep the reader away from historical, biblical moorings."[73] Hayes, interestingly, sees congruence between Pinnock's reflections on hell and Catholic theology. As a Catholic, Hayes exhorts Pinnock's point regarding hell as self-destruction. However, Hayes differs on the nature of final loss. In his words, "Is such final loss simple nonexistence? Or is it a continued subjective existence in the self-enclosed isolation one has chosen in one's historical existence?"[74] While Pinnock argues for the former, Hayes contends for the latter.

Despite such criticisms, Pinnock believes that annihilationism is the only true "third possibility" lying between everlasting torment and universalism. In his view, annihilationism makes the best sense of Scripture while also being most consistent with the God who is boundless love.

growing popularity. See Sprinkle, *Four Views on Hell*.

70. As is standard within "The Counterpoint Series" by Zondervan Publishing, each author of *Four Views on Hell* propose different assessments on what Scripture claims about hell while also responding to each other's articles.

71. Walvoord, "Response to Clark Pinnock," 170.

72. Crockett, "Response to Clark Pinnock," 171.

73. Crockett, "Response to Clark Pinnock," 174.

74. Hayes, "Response to Clark Pinnock," 177.

Bibliography

Allen, Bob. "Baptist Theologian Clark Pinnock Dies." *Christian Century* 127/19 (2010) 18.

Barr, James. "Review of *The Scripture Principle*." *Virginia Seminary Journal* (1986) 36–38.

Bloesch, Donald G. *God the Almighty: Power, Wisdom, Holiness, Love*. Downers Grove, IL: InterVarsity, 1995.

Bonhoeffer, Dietrich. *Letters and Papers from Prison*. Vol. 8. Minneapolis: Fortress, 2010.

Bryant, Odell. *Spirit Christology in the Christian Tradition: From the Patristic Period to the Rise of Pentecostalism in the Twentieth Century*. Cleveland: CPT, 2014.

Callen, Barry L. "Clark H. Pinnock: His Life and Work." In *Semper Reformandum: Studies in Honour of Clark H. Pinnock*, edited by Stanley E. Porter and Anthony R. Cross, 2–15. Milton Keyes, UK: Paternoster, 2003.

———. *Journey Toward Renewal: An Intellectual Biography*. Nappanee, IN: Evangel, 2000.

Chan, Simon. *Pentecostal Theology and the Christian Spiritual Tradition*. Eugene, OR: Wipf and Stock, 2000.

Cobb, John B., Jr. "Clark Pinnock and Process Theology." In *Semper Reformandum: Studies in Honour of Clark H. Pinnock*, edited by Stanley E. Porter and Anthony R. Cross, 261–74. Milton Keyes, UK: Paternoster, 2003.

Cobb, John B., Jr., and Clark H. Pinnock, eds. *Searching for an Adequate God: A Dialogue Between Process and Free Will Theists*. Grand Rapids: Eerdmans, 2000.

Crockett, William V. "Response to Clark Pinnock." In *Four Views on Hell*, edited by William V. Crockett, 171–74. Grand Rapids: Zondervan, 1996.

Cross, Terry. "A Critical Review of Clark Pinnock's *Flame of Love: A Theology of the Holy Spirit*." *Journal of Pentecostal Theology* 6/13 (1998) 3–29.

Edwards, David L., and John Stott. *Evangelical Essentials: A Liberal Evangelical Dialogue*. Downers Grove, IL: InterVarsity, 1989.

Gathercole, Simon J. "A Conversion of Augustine: From Natural Law to Restored Nature in Romans 2.13–16." *Seminar Papers* 135/38 (1999) 327–58.

Griffin, David Ray. "Process Theology and the Christian Good News." In *Searching for an Adequate God: A Dialogue between Process and Free Will Theists*, edited by John B. Cobb Jr. and Clark H. Pinnock, 1–38. Grand Rapids: Eerdmans, 2000.

Gunton, Colin E. *The Promise of Trinitarian Theology*. New York: T&T Clark, 1991.

Hayes, Zachary J. "Response to Clark Pinnock." In *Four Views on Hell*, edited by William V. Crockett, 175–78. Grand Rapids: Zondervan, 1996.

Hilary of Poitiers. "On the Trinity." 1.6.

Jenson, Robert W. *Systematic Theology*. Vol. 1, *The Triune God*. New York: Oxford University Press, 1999.

———. *The Triune Identity: God according to the Gospel*. Philadelphia: Fortress, 1982.

John of Damascus. "Orthodox Faith." 1.13.

Kärkkäinen, Veli-Matti. *The Holy Spirit: A Guide to Christian Theology*. Louisville: Westminster John Knox, 2012.

———. *An Introduction to the Theology of Religions: Biblical, Historical, and Contemporary Perspectives*. Downers Grove, IL: InterVarsity, 2003.

Lossky, Vladimir. *Dogmatic Theology: Creation, God's Image in Man, and the Redeeming Work of the Trinity*. Yonkers, NY: Saint Vladimir's Seminary Press, 2017.

Macchia, Frank. "Tradition and the *Novum* of the Spirit: A Review of Clark Pinnock's *Flame of Love*." *Journal of Pentecostal Theology* 6/13 (1998) 31–48.

Maddox, Randy. "Review: *The Scripture Principle*." *Wesleyan Theological Journal* 21/1–2 (1986) 204–7.

Marshall, I. Howard. "For All, for All My Saviour Died." In *Semper Reformandum: Studies in Honour of Clark H. Pinnock*," edited by Stanley E. Porter and Anthony R. Cross, 322–46. Milton Keyes, UK: Paternoster, 2003.

Moltmann, Jürgen. "God's *Kenosis* in the Creation and Consummation of the World." In *The Work of Love: Creation as Kenosis*, edited by John Polkinghorne, 137–51. Grand Rapids: Eerdmans, 2001.

———. *The Trinity and the Kingdom: The Doctrine of God*. Minneapolis: Fortress, 1981.

Nicole, Roger. "Clark Pinnock's Precarious Balance Between Openmindedness and Doctrinal Instability." *Christianity Today* 29/2 (1985) 68–71.

Olson, Roger E. "Postconservative Evangelical Theology and the Theological Pilgrimage of Clark Pinnock." In *Semper Reformandum: Studies in Honour of Clark H. Pinnock*," edited by Stanley E. Porter and Anthony R. Cross, 16–37. Milton Keyes, UK: Paternoster, 2003.

Oord, Thomas Jay. "Clark Pinnock Passes on to Glory." (blog) August 6, 2010. http://thomasjayoord.com/index.php/blog/archives/clark_pinnock_passes_on_to_glory.

Pinnock, Clark H. "Afterword." In *Journey Towards Renewal: An Intellectual Biography*, by Barry L. Callen, 269–72. Nappanee, IN: Evangel, 2000.

———. "Between Classical and Process Theism." In *Process Theology*, edited by Ronald Nash, 309–27. Grand Rapids: Baker, 1987.

———. "Biblical Texts: Past and Future Meanings." *Wesleyan Theological Journal* 34/2 (1999) 136–51.

———. "A Bridge and Some Points of Growth: A Reply to Cross and Macchia." *Journal of Pentecostal Theology* 6/13 (1998) 49–54.

———. "Church in the Power of the Spirit: The Promise of Pentecostal Ecclesiology." *Journal of Pentecostal Theology* 14/2 (2006) 147–65.

———. "Clark Pinnock's Response to Part 1." In *Reconstructing Theology: A Critical Assessment of the Theology of Clark Pinnock*, edited by Tony Gray and Christopher Sinkinson, 81–87. Carlisle, Cumbia, UK: Paternoster, 2000.

———. "Clark Pinnock's Response to Part 2." In *Reconstructing Theology: A Critical Assessment of the Theology of Clark Pinnock*, edited by Tony Gray and Christopher Sinkinson, 147–52. Carlisle, Cumbia, UK: Paternoster, 2000.

———. "Climbing Out of a Swamp: The Evangelical Struggle to Understand the Creation Texts." *Interpretation* 43/2 (1989) 143–55.

———. "Conditional View." In *Four Views on Hell*, edited by William V. Crockett, 135–66. Grand Rapids: Zondervan, 1996.

———. "Confessions of a Post-Conservative Evangelical Theologian." *Dialog* 45/4 (2006) 382–88.

———. "Constrained by Love: Divine Self-Restraint according to Open Theism." *Perspectives in Religious Studies* 34/2 (2007) 149–60.

———. "The Destruction of the Finally Impenitent." *Criswell Theological Review* 4/ 2 (1990) 243–59.

———. "Divine Relationality: A Pentecostal Contribution to the Doctrine of God." *Journal of Pentecostal Theology* 8/16 (2000) 3–26.

———. "Evangelical Theology after Darwin." In *Creation Made Free: Open Theology Engaging Science*, edited by Thomas Jay Oord, 103–10. Eugene, OR: Pickwick, 2009.

———. "Fire, Then Nothing." *Christianity Today* 31/5 (1987) 40–41.

———. *Flame of Love: A Theology of the Holy Spirit*. Downers Grove, IL: InterVarsity, 1996.

———. "Foreword." In *Clark H. Pinnock on Biblical Authority: An Evolving Position*, by Roy C. W. Roennfeldt, xv–xxiii. Berrien Springs, MI: Andrews University Press, 1993.

———. "From Augustine to Arminius: A Pilgrimage in Theology." In *The Grace of God and the Will of Man*, edited by Clark H. Pinnock, 15–30. Minneapolis: Bethany House, 1989.

———. "The Great Jubilee." In *God and Man: Perspectives on Christianity in the 20th Century*, edited by Michael Bauman, 91–102. Hillsdale, MI: Hillsdale College Press, 1995.

———. "How I Use the Bible When Doing Theology." In *The Use of the Bible in Theology: Evangelical Options*, edited by Robert K. Johnston, 18–34. Atlanta: John Knox, 1985.

———. *Most Moved Mover: A Theology of God's Openness*. Carlisle, Cumbia, UK: Paternoster, 2001.

———. "New Dimensions in Theological Method." In *New Dimensions in Evangelical Theology: Essays in Honor of Millard J. Erickson*, edited by David S. Dockery, 197–208. Downers Grove, IL: InterVarsity, 1998.

———. "The New Pentecostalism: Reflections by a Well-Wisher." *Christianity Today* 17/24 (1973) 6–10.

———. "The Other Hand of God: God's Spirit in an Age of Scientific Cosmology." *Stone-Campbell Journal* 9/2 (2006), 205–30.

———. "The Physical Side of Being Spiritual: God's Sacramental Presence." In *Baptist Sacramentalism*, edited by Anthony R. Cross and Philip E. Thompson, 8–20. Carlisle, Cumbia, UK: Paternoster, 2003.

———. "Pinnock Postscript: How My Mind Has Changed." In *Clark H. Pinnock: Journey Toward Renewal: An Intellectual Biography*, by Barry L. Callen, 228–29, 236–37. Nappanee, IN: Evangel, 2000.

———. "Relational Theology Among the Evangelicals." Paper presented at the American Academy of Religion Open and Relational Theologies Group, Denver, CO, November 2001.

———. "Response to Daniel Strange and Amos Yong." *Evangelical Quarterly* 71/4 (1999) 349–57.

———. "The Role of the Spirit in Creation." *The Asbury Theological Journal* 52/1 (1997) 47–54.

———. "The Role of the Spirit in Interpretation." *Journal of the Evangelical Theological Society* 36/4 (1993) 491–97.

———. *The Scripture Principle*. San Francisco: Harper and Row, 1984.

———. "Systematic Theology." In *The Openness of God: A Biblical Challenge to the Traditional Understanding of God*, edited by Clark H. Pinnock et. al., 101–25. Downers Grove, IL: InterVarsity, 1994.

———. *Three Keys to Spiritual Renewal*. Minneapolis: Bethany House, 1985.

———. "Toward an Evangelical Theology of Religions." *Journal of the Evangelical Theological Society* 33/2–3 (1990) 359–68.

———. *Tracking the Maze: Finding Our Way Through Modern Theology from an Evangelical Perspective*. San Francisco: Harper and Row, 1990.

———. *A Wideness in God's Mercy: The Finality of Jesus Christ in a World of Religions*. Grand Rapids: Zondervan, 1992.

———. "The Work of the Holy Spirit in Hermeneutics." *Journal of Pentecostal Theology* 1/2 (1993) 3–23.

———. "The Work of the Spirit in the Interpretation of Holy Scripture from the Perspective of a Charismatic Biblical Theologian." *Journal of Pentecostal Theology* 18/2 (2009) 157–71.

Pinnock, Clark H., and Delwin Brown. *Theological Crossfire: An Evangelical/Liberal Dialogue*. Grand Rapids: Zondervan, 1990.

Pinnock, Clark H., and Robert C. Brow. *Unbounded Love: A Good News Theology for the 21st Century*. Downers Grove, IL: InterVarsity, 1994.

Pinnock, Clark H., et. al. *The Openness of God: A Biblical Challenge to the Traditional Understanding of God*. Downers Grove, IL: InterVarsity, 2010.

Piper, John, et. al. *Beyond the Bounds: Open Theism and the Undermining of Biblical Christianity*. Wheaton, IL: Crossway, 2003.

Polkinghorne, John. *Science and Religion in the Quest of Truth*. New Haven: Yale University Press, 2011.

Sprinkle, Preston, ed. *Four Views on Hell: Second Edition*. Grand Rapids: Zondervan, 2016.

Strange, Daniel. "Biographical Essay: Clark H. Pinnock: The Evolution of an Evangelical." In *Reconstructing Theology: A Critical Assessment of the Theology of Clark Pinnock*, edited by Tony Gray and Christopher Sinkinson, 1–20. Carlisle, Cumbia, UK: Paternoster, 2000.

———.*The Possibility of Salvation Among the Unevangelized: An Analysis of Inclusivism in Recent Evangelical Theology*. Eugene, OR: Wipf and Stock, 2007.

———. "Presence, Prevenience, or Providence? Deciphering the Conundrum of Pinnock's Pneumatological Inclusivism.'" In *Reconstructing Theology: A Critical Assessment of the Theology of Clark Pinnock*, edited by Tony Gray and Christopher Sinkinson, 220–58. Carlisle, Cambria, UK: Paternoster, 2000.

Studebaker, Steven M. "Clark H. Pinnock: Charismatic Pilgrim." *Canadian Journal of Pentecostal-Charismatic Christianity* 1/1 (2010) 1–30.

———. *From Pentecost to the Triune God: A Pentecostal Trinitarian Theology*. Grand Rapids: Eerdmans, 2012.

———. "Integrating Pneumatology and Christology: A Trinitarian Modification of Clark H. Pinnock's Spirit Christology." *Pneuma: The Journal of the Society for Pentecostal Studies* 28/1 (2006) 5–20.

Swoboda, A. J. *Tongues and Trees: Towards a Pentecostal Ecological Theology*. Blandford Forum, UK: Deo, 2013.

Thomas, John Christopher. "Editorial: Clark Pinnock." *Journal of Pentecostal Theology* 20/1 (2011) 1–3.

Walvoord, John F. "Response to Clark Pinnock." In *Four Views on Hell*, edited by William V. Crockett, 167–70. Grand Rapids: Zondervan, 1996.

Ware, Bruce A. "Defining Evangelicalism's Boundaries Theologically: Is Open Theism Evangelical?" The *Journal of the Evangelical Theological Society* 45/2 (2002) 193–212.

———. *God's Lesser Glory: The Diminished God of Open Theism*. Wheaton, IL: Crossway, 2000.

Williams, Rowan. *On Christian Theology*. Malden: Blackwell, 2000.

Wolterstorff, Nicholas. "God Everlasting." In *Contemporary Philosophy of Religion*, edited by Steven M. Cahn and David Shatz, 181–203. New York: Oxford University Press, 1982.

Yong, Amos. "Whither Theological Inclusivism?: The Development and Critique of an Evangelical Theology of Religions." *Evangelical Quarterly* 71/4 (1999) 327–48.

Zizioulas, John. *Being as Communion: Studies in Personhood and the Church*. Yonkers, NY: St. Vladimir's Seminary Press, 1985.

Name Index